Advance Praise

"Mary Lea Carroll's travels, irrepressible curiosity, and mischievous sense of humor range far and wide. Battles? Who cares? Let's get to the interesting stuff: Relics! Bones! She brings us complex people of faith who worked to alleviate the suffering of—or were themselves—poor, marginalized, and/or people of color. She interjects just enough personal history so we can sense the depth of her own quest. And she infuses the stories of these 'somehow saints' with wit, warmth, and heart."

— HEATHER KING,
columnist and author of *Holy Desperation:
Praying as If Your Life Depends on It*

"Traveling with Mary Lea Carroll is like vacationing with a witty friend who educates you as you go. You won't even realize how much you're learning because you'll be so busy having a good time. Book this book as you would a great trip."

— CHRIS ERSKINE,
Los Angeles Times columnist and author of *Daditude*

Praise for
Saint Everywhere

A *PEOPLE* Magazine Pick

Southern California Independent Bookseller Award Finalist

"Spiritual, funny, and full of heart. Works as a travel guide or pick-me-up if you're seeking some kind of salvation."
— THE SATELLITE SISTERS

"Charming, funny, informative, moving, and spiritually profound."
— MICHELLE HUNEVEN,
author of *Blame* and *Round Rock*

"[A] delightful piece of narrative nonfiction.... Writing in an utterly unaffected tone and bringing a resonant universality to her musings, [Carroll] invites readers to come along [with her].... Different religions notwithstanding, most readers will be all in for this journey—learning, enjoying, and pondering in equal measure."
— *Booklist*

"Carroll's gift to readers isn't just her charming tale of her travels and the lives of women who did what Carroll refers to as 'grand, eternal things,' but her own story of realizing that it's never too late to make your dreams come true."
— *Orange County Register*

"With the effortless, heartfelt wit of Annie Lamott, Mary Lea Carroll whisks us along on a series of lively, serendipitous pilgrimages that leave us laughing, amazed, and ready to set off on our own miraculous adventures."
— PERDITA FINN,
coauthor of *The Way of the Rose*

Somehow Saints

MORE TRAVELS IN SEARCH OF THE SAINTLY

MARY LEA CARROLL

ILLUSTRATIONS BY JOE ROHDE

Prospect Park Books

Published by Prospect Park Books
2359 Lincoln Avenue
Altadena, California 91001
www.prospectparkbooks.com

Distributed by Consortium Book Sales & Distribution
www.cbsd.com

Library of Congress Cataloging-in-Publication Data

Names: Carroll, Mary Lea, author.
Title: Somehow saints : more travels in search of the saintly / Mary
    Lea Carroll.
Description: Altadena, California : Prospect Park Books, [2020]
Identifiers: LCCN 2020022893 (print) | LCCN 2020022894 (ebook) |
    ISBN 9781945551895 (hardback) | ISBN 9781945551901 (epub)
Subjects: LCSH: Christian women saints. | Christian shrines. |
    Christian pilgrims and pilgrimages.
Classification: LCC BR1713 .C369 2020 (print) | LCC BR1713
    (ebook) | DDC 270.092/52--dc23
LC record available at https://lccn.loc.gov/2020022893
LC ebook record available at https://lccn.loc.gov/2020022894

Illustrations by Joe Rohde
Cover photo of St. Josephine Bakhita mural by Andrew Heavens
Cover design by David Ter-Avanesyan
Page design & layout by Amy Inouye, Future Studio

Printed in Canada

"There is no saint without a past, no sinner without a future."

— St. Augustine (most likely)

For
Jane Ray

Contents

Light the Lamps!

On my sixty-third birthday, I committed to a wild, wishful desire. A kind of defiant act, wanting the years ahead to have bigger meaning. If one is lucky enough to live to ninety, all these late-in-life years have to have more going for them than simply checking in on the kids and trying to…what? Not gain weight? Not eat dinner too early? Not wear clothes that are twenty years old? I committed to something that had stayed in hiding for most of my life: writing a book. *Too hard. Others are way smarter. Who needs another book?* But through constant prayer of "What, Lord, what shall I make of my life at this age?" a little flame got sparked. I began to think quite differently. If, indeed, it is God's desire to give us *our* heart's desire, then who am I to deny it? And if not me, then who? Are we not each one hundred percent unique? So with a morning prayer of, "Please, Lord, don't make it too hard. I'm not that good at hard," I put my fingers to the keyboard. I made one demand upon myself—two, really: 1. I would finish it; and 2. I would do everything in my power to get it out into the world, even if it meant standing on the street wearing a sandwich sign.

With the publication in 2019 of *Saint Everywhere— Travels in Search of the Lady Saints*, a new life chapter opened up: speaking engagements and promotional book travels that took me to several cities across the country. These activities put me on a type of self-improvement program. What I looked like, being on time, and being prepared became important. Most importantly, I couldn't allow myself to give in to thoughts of insecurity. To go from working away quietly at my desk on an eccentric project that might lie there forever, like so many before it, to having a book come full fruit into the public has been, to put it mildly, a completely wild trip!

Upon completing *Saint Everywhere*, the writing about saints felt complete. I'd reached and created to the best of my abilities. But one of the blessings of speaking to so many readers was the encouragement I received for more: "More saints, more fun stories, more."

So with the invitation of my publisher to write a second book, I thought, *Better get traveling*. Wait—I already *was* traveling, crisscrossing the United States, reading in bookstores, libraries, and churches, and speaking at home parties. It occurred to me that I could begin my search for *Somehow Saints* in the city *Saint Everywhere* was already taking me to, Washington, DC. Surely there would be inspiring saints within easy train rides. At the same time, I was realizing that I had a few things to share about my childhood.

Throughout my adult life, friends have asked for the stories I tell about growing up in a big, loose household in the '60s. We were nine brothers and sisters, half of us Irish twins to each another. Every night, my mother cooked for twelve in a kitchen big enough for two dining tables. The yard was so full of kids that people wondered if it might be a school. But no, it was just us, with our friends over. My grandmother, an old silent-movie star, lived with us; how we laughed every time she backed out of the driveway, taking half the hedge with her. That big ol' house on Santa Rosa Street in Altadena, California, which got its name changed every December to Christmas Tree Lane, sheltered us and all our shenanigans.

As I stand on the threshold of old age, the time the French say is the time to reflect, I can't seem to keep some of those stories out of my mind. In this book, they're mixed in as a yin to the yang of the tales of my "somehow saints"—a name that stands for all of us, even those who actually made it to full-on sainthood.

Each of us seems to be carrying the weight of the world on our shoulders these days. The lives of these somehow saints amaze and encourage us. They carried loads far greater than anything most of us will experience, and they give us perspective. Even as I write this, with such a swift change in reality as a global health crisis impedes our travel, shaking us to the core, the stories of these saints bolster us for the road we tread. These remarkable, one-in-a-million people dot all eras and all cultures. They're a reminder that no matter how dark the darkness, it cannot extinguish the light of one candle. And the lights that they are tell us we, too, are candles.

So, with joy, let's have another go at the world, for discoveries large and small of the goodness in our midst, created by those living and those who will live forever through their deeds. Valiant saints and helpers, light the lamps! You've got visitors.

One

Off-Roading in America

ST. KATHARINE DREXEL
1858–1955
Philadelphia and the American West and South

How fun to plot out a train trip back East. Already in DC to give copies of *Saint Everywhere* to the chapter reps of the National Christ Child Society, I could, after that, go anywhere. My feet bounced in my shoes as I studied Amtrak's website. There's Philadelphia. Only been there once. Oh, look, there's a route right up to Canada. I've never been to Canada…would there be saints to fall in love with on such a route?

But gosh, after spending a whole morning on the Amtrak site, I just needed a real person on the phone.

"Agent! Agent!" I enunciated clearly into Amtrak's call system. After being asked for a great deal of nonpertinent information, the unhelpful robot switched me to the "customer service" robot. There I was looped back and forth, giving the same information I'd just given the first nonhelper. This got me to almost shouting "Agent! Agent!" hoping to break through. And then "Julie" came on. *Are all these customer-care robots named Julie?* She couldn't tell me how many stops there were between New York City and Montreal. She was silent on the question as to whether there was a quiet car. *Julie,* can I reserve a seat? She didn't know. I was practically in tears with frustration, but then *real-life* Nancy came on! She had such a soothing voice that I didn't trust it. Had AI recognized my tone and switched on the robot for problem customers? "Nancy! Are you a real person?" I demanded. She laughed.

"Yes, ma'am. What can I do for you this evening?" Her voice was warm and mellow. I let out a sigh. But still, could I be sure?

"Just a little bit of information on your DC-Philadelphia-Montreal route."

"Okay," she said. "What would you like to know?"

And now here I was! Happily standing in one of the great railway stations in the country, DC's Union Station. Its architecture is so frescoed, so grand—a thrilling start to my train travels. There'd be two and a half hours to look out the window at the things seldom seen from freeways. The back sides of wrecking yards and old factories. So many interesting polluted canals. In Philadelphia, my aim was to learn more about Katharine Drexel, the fabulous society heiress who became a saint.

Very few inspiring people had the array of life

choices Katharine Drexel did. At the age of twenty-five, she and her two sisters inherited $14 million, quite a fortune in 1883. There are photos of her as a little girl wearing a coat edged in ermine. Photos of her in a summer dress, with her horse, Roland, driving the lanes near their summer house. Her father and her uncle had made their money in finance during the Gold Rush and the Civil War. What was expected of Katharine was to make a brilliant marriage match and take her place among her peers. But what she *did do* was cast her eyes upon the most mistreated and forgotten segments of society: African Americans and Native Americans. These were the "others" with whom white people didn't want to interact with. For this, some call her the Mother Teresa of America. In that era, from 1890 through the 1940s, Katherine had the chutzpah and personality to attract hundreds of women to join her as she off-roaded across America, pioneering the advancement of racial equality and education.

I climbed aboard Amtrak and headed to the city of brotherly love to learn more about a woman who had enough love for all humanity.

As a young adult, Katharine took herself and her future very seriously. She knew that because of her wealth, what she did mattered. She gave herself personal progress reports on her own conduct: Was she praying enough? Had she been helpful enough to those around her? Shouldn't she, really, be doing much more?

Oh, to have set better goals when I was young! But even well past college, I was batting around San Francisco as a tour guide, a ghostwriter, a waitress.

It's said that the family is the classroom for a person's values. With a chuckle, I thought of my own childhood family values—like, for starters, better hide your candy. It was our money, as in *I'll give you one Snickers if you help me band my newspapers*. Success meant getting someone to laugh. With nine of us brothers and sisters, humor could get you out of anything. Oh my gosh, the way Mom—I've taken to calling her Good St. Jane—started her day was this: First, she'd heft herself up to a sitting position in bed and call out, loud and pleadingly, "Coffee...somebody?...coffee?" until one of us in the kitchen heard her. Next, she'd reach for her Valium. Things got so much better for all of us once mood drugs came on the market. Then, she'd light her first cigarette. By that time, one of us kids would have mixed the coffee crystals into a cup of hot water and arrived with it. She'd accept it like a thirsty person. And after she'd had her moment of me-time and everything had kicked in, she was "up like a gazelle" for her morning writing assignment. Mom always wanted to be a writer. Her assignment went like this: She'd spread nine brown bags out on the counter, get a pencil, and write *Jimmy, Sally, Jeffrey, Dan, Mary Lea, Kevin, John, Beth,* and *Mark* across the top of each one. In went a bologna sandwich, an apple, a cookie. Every day for a couple of decades.

The values Katharine learned at home were different: Money was for social service, prayer was absolutely central to each day, and civic engagement was your duty. I shook my head, almost laughing to myself as I read more about her childhood. My brother Jeff saw civic engagement as his duty, too—his duty to wear out-landish clothes, get himself arrested at LAX, and end up on the front page of the *Los Angeles Times* for wearing the flag as a poncho. It was 1968. My poor mom got a flood of calls from her sympathetic girlfriends whose kids were also done with authority.

Every Catholic parish in Philadelphia benefited from the Drexels' generosity. They had an oratory for nightly prayer built onto their home. Bishops were frequent visitors. Katharine's father, Francis Drexel, sat on charitable boards, and these charities were often topics at family dinnertime. Katharine's mother, Emma, handled the constant stream of people at their front and back doors needing food or clothing or asking for odd jobs. She served all who came her way and even sent her assistant into the tenements to hunt for families in dire need. The Drexel girls—Katharine, Louise, and Elizabeth—absorbed this, each in her own way.

It was Katharine who nursed her mother for three years until she died from cancer in 1883. Emma's death was crushing to the family. So, the next year, Francis took his daughters on a trip west, figuring that the ruggedness and fresh air would be good for them all. Yes, the territories were inspiring and majestic, but seeing firsthand the misery on the Indian reservations they passed through struck Katharine's heart. The infertile barrenness of the land, the eradication of buffalo, the unfulfilled government promises for schools and infrastructure, the alcoholism, the social breakdown—all this began a fire in her, a righteous fire. At home in Philadelphia, she had for some time been raising funds as a lay mission helper to the Jesuits, but her trip west opened her eyes to a suffering she had been unaware of.

I'd be in Philly in fifteen minutes and took to standing between cars, rocking back and forth, afraid for no good reason that I'd miss my stop. It's a pitfall of traveling alone, the fear that you might do something stupid. But right on time, I and my roller bag hopped off. Philadelphia, great! It's a city of 1.5 million and so darn old—founded in 1682! I love that the word *Philadelphia* is Greek and actually does mean *the city of brotherly love*. I knew that, but I didn't know the Greek part. Philadelphia is the very birthplace of the founding of this country. It has the bell, the Constitution, and the "Rocky steps" of the Philadelphia Museum of Art, which is among the top museums anywhere.

Straightaway, I caught a cab to the Cathedral Basilica of saints Peter and Paul. This is where Katharine worshipped as a little girl. I bumped my suitcase up the steps and rolled it through the open bronze doors. Inside, the beauty made my hand go to my heart as I took in all the gold and Renaissance-inspired grandeur. They sure knew how to build churches in the 1800s.

I found the side chapel I was looking for, with its marble railings, statuary, and a few rows of pews. Simply engraved across the front of the white granite tomb: *Reverend Mother Mary Katharine Drexel*. To me, the simplicity spelled the importance not just of her but of her family to Philadelphia. I knelt down. I felt small. She was real, and I was at her tomb. *Help me "fear nothing and press on," as you did*, I prayed. *St. Katharine, you stood up against people cursing at you, but you just were not afraid.* Jesus continually told us to be not afraid. Be not afraid...yet it seems media, friends, and the world say the opposite.

After her father died and she got her inheritance, Katharine was thrown into personal chaos. In her journal, she wrote that she did not want a life of "comfortable insignificance." But what to do with herself? What to do with her wealth? What was her responsibility to society? Was she up to a religious calling? Well, to try to find an answer, she did what wealthy girls did in the Gilded Age. She and her sisters took themselves off to Europe.

Like in the movie *A Room with a View*, Katharine and her sisters visited museums and took the medicinal waters, but really what she did was go see the pope. If your last name was Drexel, you could do that sort of thing. She wanted Pope Leo XIII to know how terrible conditions were for African Americans and Native Americans. She begged him to send help to them. This was the same pope who'd later grant Mother Francis Cabrini permission to be a missionary to the Italians in New York. Katharine spoke to him on three separate occasions, each talk ending with her quandary and confusion about her own life's purpose. Finally, the pope said, "You, Katharine—you yourself become that missionary." According to her diary, when she left that audience, she was sick to her stomach. She cried and cried. Yet she knew it was the answer. But it scared her.

Later, in her discernment process to determine whether she could or would become a nun, she listed her worries. "I have never been deprived of luxuries."

"How could I bear separation from my family?" "I hate community life." She wrote that mother superiors "are frequently selected on their holiness, *not* for ability. I should hate to owe submission to a woman whom I felt to be stupid."

Well, she worked it out. Along with the regular vows of chastity, poverty, and obedience, Katharine added a fourth: "To be the mother and servant of the Indian and Negro races." (She used the words *Negro*, *Colored*, and *Indian*, always capitalized, as was the norm at that time.) It's funny: I know women who never had children because they felt they didn't have enough to give. Yet there are other women, like Katharine, who feel they have enough to give for all humanity. On a small level, my own mother said having one baby was the biggest shock to your identity possible. The first one breaks you down, allowing room for all the others who come along....

Katharine had a plan. After receiving her training, she would start her own order. This way, she could control her own money. That was the deal she made with the Church, because otherwise, given the prejudices and sexism of the time, it wouldn't get spent the way she wanted. And while luxuries had never been denied her, she began in earnest to deny them to herself. She embraced kenotic spirituality, an emptying of one's self to allow the room to be filled with the will of God. That required a "poverty of spirit": rejecting comforts, fasting, and giving over to penance mortifications. I am at a loss to understand why mortifying the flesh was ever a good thing. I know people once had a solid answer to this, but why would we harm our bodies by spike belts and discipline switches? I believe these practices are almost gone today, but even reading about it is upsetting. Are we not to love and tend to the well-being of our body as the precious vessel for our mind and spirit that it is?

By 1894, 112 women had been attracted to Katharine's fledgling order, the Sisters of the Blessed Sacrament. She imbued her order with a special devotion to the Virgin Mary, and thus all of her sisters adopted the name Mary. Sister Mary Katharine Drexel, Sister Mary Agatha, Sister Mary Patrick, and so on. "Earthly mothers are imperfect and can give way to their bad humor and sometimes scold their children; while Mary knows only how to console, to relieve, to purify," Katharine said. Her sisters were to be that kind of mother to people who were suffering.

Yes, earthly mothers certainly could lose it! Once Mom got so mad at my brother Jeff and his scruffy, hippie friends for hanging around the house all bleary-eyed that she broke down and screamed, "All of you get out!" Then she spun around and banged *me* over the head with a cookie sheet!

"Why me?" I cried.

"You're—you're closer!" she yelled.

My mother had been a dutiful only child, and her life with us had put her on a steep learning curve. After we had gone to bed and Dad was asleep, I remember seeing her sometimes, late, kneeling by the bed and saying the rosary.

Early on, Katharine built a boarding school "for

Negro girls" attached to the mother house of her order in Bensalem, Pennsylvania. Katharine and her order were labeled troublemakers from the start. A stick of dynamite was found at the boarding school's construction site as a warning to her to quit. Thank goodness it was discovered before the dedication ceremony or she and several others might have been killed.

Undaunted, and soon after that, in 1894, Katharine and four missionary sisters headed out to Santa Fe, New Mexico. While she'd been funding missions for more than ten years, St. Catherine's in Santa Fe was the first mission she started from the ground up. There is a photo of a buckboard full of nuns traveling the five hours it took to cross the desert from the Albuquerque train station to Santa Fe—funny but inspiring—five nuns riding in full black, stuffy robes across such forbidding, barren land. They were from the cluttered, busy cities of the East and had entered country that sort of hurts so good. Make a wrong move, get lost, and you die. But where else could sunsets and landforms offer such vast magnificence?

Next, she set her eyes on the South. In 1899, Katharine bought an abandoned plantation outside of Richmond, Virginia, and turned it into St. Francis, a boarding academy for African American girls; she opened St. Emma's next door for boys. These two academies would teach students for the next seventy years. Next, in 1902, she opened St. Michael's in Mission, Arizona, to educate Navajo children; it continues to thrive today. Then, in 1905, came the Academy of the Immaculate Mother in Nashville, Tennessee, where some girls were trained to become teachers and others took a full course of domestic science and dressmaking.

It added up. Over the next forty years, Katharine and her growing band of sisters would establish forty-nine elementary and high schools for African Americans and twelve schools for Native Americans. SBS schools, as they became known, emphasized producing as many teachers as possible. This was Katharine's way of elevating an entire group of people who had been repressed. She financially supported or founded 145 missions, which were centers for prayer, education, and help, from Oklahoma to Tucson and from Richmond, Virginia, to Beaumont, Texas. She founded Xavier University of Louisiana, the only historically black Catholic university in the country. To this day, Xavier sends more students of color to medical schools than any other university in the country. She founded the first teacher-training department at Catholic University in DC and sent her sisters to summer school for higher degrees. It was an innovation to have teachers trained at this high level.

Katharine did not integrate her own order because the fledgling black orders of Catholic sisters, the Oblates and the Sisters of the Holy Family, asked her not to, as it would weaken their fragile development. Eventually, many years later, the SBS did integrate.

In Katharine's lifetime, the Blessed Sacrament Sisters for Indians and Colored People (full title) grew to be 600 strong. These women were certain that the way to improve the lives of those in deep poverty was to build up their strength by bringing them to God's love.

That, and education. You educate one girl or one boy, she or he brings that education home, and that home brings it to society.

Katharine had to work against or around the laws. When she was building a church in rural Virginia, for example, officials stopped construction because she hadn't built a "colored section" in back. She refused to relegate African American worshippers to the back, so she redesigned the church. It caused a fight, but she got her new plan through. With a white side and a black side (African Americans on their side up front), it was still segregation, but it was progress.

Windows got smashed in her Catholic schools because white society was unnerved by white women teachers mixing with black children. The sisters were cursed at, called "n----- sisters," and threatened by the Ku Klux Klan. Katharine used sham companies to buy real estate, lest city fathers get wind of another SBS school. In many places—including Chicago, Louisiana, the Dakotas, and New Mexico—the SBS did it alone, without Church support. Bishops either threw up their hands, turned a blind eye, or abetted the existing Jim Crow laws.

Although so uncertain as a young woman, Katharine Drexel later came to know exactly what her mission was on earth. Sister Mary John recalled walking with Mother Katharine one afternoon when the founder said, "Sister, we will do this work until the conscience of America is awakened." She is credited with bringing integration and social justice to the forefront of the Church's agenda. Bishops were talking about it, but Katharine and her sisters were *doing* it. To her, there were no differences between people. She actually did what all of us are called to do: See the face of God in each of our fellows. And she saw suffering. If Katharine were alive today, I doubt she would be able to walk past a homeless person passed out on the sidewalk. No, she'd have an eighteen-wheeler following her around that was fitted out as a hospital.

I left the cathedral to go find my hotel. The air was cold and bracing. I'd walk the mile and a half. Philadelphia is certainly Katherine's town. A large bronze statue of her uncle Anthony sits on top of a ten-foot pillar on Market Street. He founded Drexel University and was a founding member of what we today call Wall Street. Throughout her life, he was her close adviser. Her sister Louise also backed many of her endeavors. Elizabeth died young, in childbirth. Twenty-seven percent of women used to die in childbirth. My own great-grandmother died in her twenties from it.

The name Drexel lit up the top of a fifteen-story building near my hotel. And apparently the light never dims as, no matter how I tried to block the window, D-R-E-X-E-L shined through all night long! (Given my interests, this made for a very weird night's sleep. *Katharine, what are you trying to say?*)

The next day I set off to find St. Katharine's archives. Abou, from Mali, took me north in his Uber through increasingly hardscrabble Philly. We passed block after block of brick row houses with rotting front doors and furniture strewn about. Empty store-fronts. I was going far away from the safety of bustling downtown. But every now and then, a solid stretch of spiffed-up houses, humming with optimism, encour-aged me to keep on. We arrived at the address for her archives. It was an empty Catholic school complex. Vast asphalt parking lot. A well-maintained but locked school. A locked church. A house, also seemingly emp-ty, sprouted out of the asphalt with a small statue of Mary by the door. Abou (whose name means "beauty and glow of face" in Arabic) waited, without my asking him to, while I checked around, everywhere, to see if a door would open. It was so lonely and quiet. My anx-iety began to rise. What was I *doing* here? Was this a parish and school that had gone bankrupt? Anxious-ly, I pressed several security buttons, and then finally Kevin, the archive manager, appeared. I waved good-bye to Abou, grateful that he'd waited.

The archive's foyer and half dozen or so rooms were quiet—echoey, actually. Kevin himself was sub-dued and preoccupied. Where had I landed? Glass display cases held curious collections: a slew of Cold War cartoons about the A-bomb. Nineteenth-century anti-Catholic cartoons from *Harpers* magazine—the long arm of the pope and such. Large dolls, almost American Girl style, showing the changing black habit of SBS nuns through the decades.

"Would you like to see the vault room first?" he asked. "I would!" I said. Though much of it was be-hind glass, I saw the saint's small leather-topped desk. Her childhood *Mother Goose* book. The dusty pink club chair her father died in. And if you have 'em, may as well show'em: six of Katharine's teeth, pulled out in 1935. Then, amazingly, a small couch that Katharine and Mother Frances Cabrini sat on together, with a picture of them hanging above it. I love it! Cabrini gave Drexel tips on how to deal with the Vatican bureaucracy and patriarchy. Did the two future saints have tea and cookies? Compare their various real estate deals? Lament the wrongs around them?

Kevin showed me how to access the more than 800 boxes of letters, photographs, deeds, and documents of St. Mother Katharine Drexel's life. I had just a few hours. I sat at a table in an empty room, and he brought a trolley cart stacked with filing boxes. I took a breath and just began opening them.

What I saw: the letter Katharine wrote imploring President Franklin Delano Roosevelt to sign an anti-lynching bill. Letters to her nuns asking them to do the same. Strangely, there were ID cards for Ku Klux Klan members. Pamphlets explaining how it's not okay to name sports teams after Indian tribes. The 1930s conference notes on the formation of the Black Catholics Association. Notes from an American bishops' conference on the Church's role in ingraining racism, noting that "conversion through coercion is not holy." Letters to Walter White, leader of the NAACP, supporting the organization and its goals. Lots of photos: Katharine picnicking with a group of Navajo under a tree, Katharine holding the hand of a small black girl with terribly deformed legs, Katharine at the Chinle, Arizona, trading post with several men, some in rancher clothes and some wrapped in Indian blankets.

She'd comb through newspapers looking for unjust and racist stories. She'd shoot back her views to the editors. Here were typed copies of the letters on fragile, yellowed onionskin. I saw a part of the civil rights movement emerging, a nascent view of a multicultural society, all through the archives of one woman.

I've had the privilege just a few times in my life to touch history. When I spoke with our friend Michael's mother, a Holocaust survivor, about her childhood experiences. When I met my friend Tina's sister, Carlotta, who was one of the Little Rock Nine. I felt that sense here, in personally handling St. Katharine Drexel's correspondence. But it also made me feel bleary-eyed and heavy, all alone in this empty space. What weight and pain to the history in my hands.

My three hours were up. I called another Uber and got a ride back to bustling downtown Philadelphia and my hotel, aptly named The Study. Food trucks lined the curb, thanks to its location between two university powerhouses: U Penn, with 24,000 students, and Drexel, with 25,000. I ate a burrito, went up to my room, and fell into a deep sleep, drenched in the long span of Katharine's life—1858 to 1955. Have you ever toured an almost-forgotten historic home that's mostly locked up and moldy smelling? In going from room to room, could you almost hear the walls talking—almost see the ghostly inhabitants? I awoke in that kind of haze.

I bundled up and went out into the cold for a solid

hour's walk, and then came back to settle myself in the lobby, which was dolled up to resemble a study, with easy chairs, library lamps, and sharpened pencils in jars. A little corny but perfect. I began to write.

Churches and schools with even the most remote connection to SBS were blocked, targeted, or destroyed before they could open. Katharine was undeterred. Macon, Georgia, passed a law to keep SBS sisters out of town; she fought that law and won. When people found out that Xavier University in Louisiana was to be for black students, they smashed out every window. After the completion of the modern, beautifully designed buildings, one of the priests at the dedication looked around and said, "What a shame." Meaning, what a waste.

Katharine and her sisters crisscrossed this country by train, boat, stagecoach, and car to bring betterment to those whom few others would aid. Her motto was to "attract them with joy," and she'd quote Jeremiah 29:7 to her sisters: "Seek the welfare of the city...for in its welfare you will find your welfare." Yes, yes, and yes.

We could all use a friend like Katharine. She paid for everything! The construction of the schools. The salaries for teachers. The saddles for the horses. The rooms and tuition for boarders. The wine for the altars. But in 1924 alone, Katharine paid $24,000 in taxes. This irritated her so much that she lobbied Congress— and won. Nicknamed the Philadelphia Nun Tax Loophole Bill, the law stated that if ninety percent of one's income is given to charity, it shall not be taxed. This was repealed in the '70s because, as you can imagine, corporations figured out how to take merciless advantage of it.

Katharine spent money so freely on others, but personally? She used pencils down to the eraser. She wrote on the insides of envelopes. She always carried her "poverty bag"—a cold sandwich and a jar of coffee—never wanting to spend money on herself. She embodied Teresa of Avila's dictum: "Be gentle to all and stern with yourself."

In her last twenty years, Katharine was confined to a wheelchair in the upper rooms of the mother house in Bensalem. Well, not actually a wheelchair—she wouldn't spend money on a real wheelchair. She had someone rig up a school desk with wheels. That's all she wanted. Needing rest after a serious heart attack, she spent those years in prayer, meditation, and letter writing. Her days of working for racial justice in the backwaters, the canyons, the inner cities were over. Much of the end of her life she simply spent in silence.

It seems to me that each person, at their core, is such a mystery. Why did Katharine push herself so hard? I believe she simply continually tested herself. Could today be better than yesterday? Can I take action today so tomorrow is an improvement? Right now, this moment, is the stepping-stone to one hour from now. Katharine did not push herself, I believe, to ultimately build all those schools or educate upward of a million students. She pushed herself to increase her capacity to love and to feel and to experience others as the face of God.

Katharine wrote in her diaries that she found her source of love for the oppressed through the Eucharist, which for Catholics is the embodiment of Jesus. She had each of her sisters spend half an hour in the morning in Eucharistic adoration in order to strengthen them for the day ahead. She had them do the same thing in the evening, to soothe and calm them after the tasks of the day. Eucharistic adoration is simply being quietly present before the blessed host, which is put in a special crystal case and then available for all to see. Some people might pray, others might fall asleep, some might make lofty plans or work out a mental worry. It's a soothing practice. After all, it isn't easy being Jesus's hands and feet in the world, even though that is what we're asked to do.

A final word from St. Katharine Drexel:

*If we wish to serve God and love our neighbor well...
press forward and fear nothing.*

Dr. Peggy

I was racing to meet Peggy for coffee. And even though Glennie, Grace, and Rosie are long grown up, their pediatrician, Dr. Peggy, and I remain friends. We got into the habit of having coffee together back in 2002, when our girls ended up at the same high school. So accomplished yet possessing so little ego, she is the kind of person with whom you find yourself just *being* with, without barriers. Even in simple catch-up conversations, I always learn so much. Want the best way to wash your hands? Need to know the actual difference between ibuprofen and acetaminophen? But mostly we laugh and we marvel at the growth of our adult daughters. We find ourselves interested in each other's wider families. It makes me happy to see her.

Over her thirty years in practice here in Pasadena, she's had more than 5,000 patients. Peggy and her husband, also a pediatrician, look after the health of all these children. She soothes the worries of all those parents. She gets up in the middle of the night to counsel over the phone or meet parents at the hospital. In fact, she came to see *me* in the hospital the day Rosie was born, to check in on her newest little patient.

"Don't make me sound like anything but a person enjoying herself," she said when I asked if I could include her in these pages. "I love what I do! I get to be involved with people through the most dramatic time of life, birth to eighteen. I get to help parents, who seem so strong and in charge, but sometimes they just dissolve in my office—'I haven't slept in two weeks!' 'I can't make her stop crying.' 'Help me; how come he's so angry?' "

My grandmother Ruthie once gave me two pieces of advice: "Only make friends with people you admire. And every time you hear a word you don't know, go home and look it up." Because she did this, no one could tell that Ruthie hadn't been educated past the third grade.

I feel like this with Dr. Peggy. I go home and think about what she says: having a life in which, basically, you feel honored to do your job. A life where she, one woman, has actually known and cared for more than 5,000 children. A busy woman who's never too busy to stop for coffee. An important woman who would never put that on display. I am reminded how much we have to learn from our friends.

Two

Light Footsteps in the Forest

ST. KATERI TEKAKWITHA
1656–1680
Upstate New York and Canada

The only reassurance real, live Nancy at Amtrak had given me about the thirteen-hour train trip to Montreal was that she was a very nice person and maybe that meant it would be a very nice train ride, too. Thin reassurance, because all the TripAdvisor reviews had said, *Beware! Bring your own food! Sit far away from the bathrooms! People are so loud!* Several reviews simply said, *Drive!*

"No, Mary Lea, we do not offer blankets," said Nancy. "No, Mary Lea, there is no quiet car. No seat assignments. Um...my screen doesn't let me know how many stops...I'm sorry." All Nancy's answers were negatory. But, shoot, how could it be worse than that summer my brother Kevin and I took trains throughout Mexico, decades ago? So often they headed backward for the first hour. How could it be worse than the time I took the Greyhound from San Francisco to Richmond, Virginia? We broke down in Fresno for a whole day. All those crazy trips in my youth. How could it be worse than hitchhiking in Morocco, sitting on a sack of vegetables!

Well, here I was sitting on Amtrak, loving the Hudson River as it flowed by, and embracing the saying, *The secret to happiness is having low expectations.* Hey, I had a thermos of good coffee and a bag of Trader Joe's healthy snacks, and the bathrooms didn't stink. Seat next to me, empty. The rhythm of the rails, the autumn forests whizzing past, watching storm clouds form all put me in a state of bliss—thirteen hours of wonderful. Funny, I've been to Hong Kong and Marrakesh but never to Montreal, and it's right next door. In Montreal, I was looking forward to learning all about a new saint whose name I could not pronounce.

Tekakwitha: The One Who Bumps into Things. That's what they called young Kateri because of her bad eyesight. When she was four, smallpox swept through her village, killing her mother, father, and brother, leaving her orphaned, partially blinded, and covered with permanent scars. Okay, I've heard of better beginnings.

Despite these obstacles—or perhaps because of them—Kateri grew up to be a young woman of compelling spiritual and mystical powers. While alive, she was admired and loved by not just her fellow Christian Iroquois but also by the missionary Jesuits, who commented about her in their letters and diaries. At the moment of her death, her larger reputation began to grow, and today she is looked to by increasing numbers around the world, especially since her saint-hood in 2012.

I'd done some research on where her shrine was, on tribal lands outside of Montreal, so that was my destination. Before too long, voilà, Montreal! It was pouring rain. I caught a cab to the hotel. My darling husband, Bill, who increasingly prefers to stay home, was arriving later, flying from LA. A quiet bar off the lobby held the promise of a nice glass of wine. It *had* been a long day of keeping to myself. Pierre, the bartender, charmed me with a *Bonsoir, madame* as I took a seat. French! They speak French! (Well, yes, for like 450 years already.) He was happy to offer a glass of wine to someone from California. I was happy just to hear him speaking French to his coworkers. Soon Pierre was hearing all about how great Amtrak was, about the progression of autumn colors as I traveled north, about Lake Champlain and the smuggling that still goes on, ever since Revolutionary War days, be-cause who can patrol the whole lake? I'd overheard that tidbit from a tour guide named Jim, who had a group of AARP travelers on the train. Soon I was deep into telling Pierre about all my travels in search of lady saints. Maybe thirteen hours was too long for me to go without talking. But Peppe—he'd invited me to call him Peppe by now—kept listening.

"Okay, well, Peppe, tomorrow I'm going out to St. Kateri's shrine. And, of course, the Oratory later."

"Really?" he said, suddenly more interested. "St. Brother André, the Oratory?" I nodded. "You must go."

"I plan to."

"You *must*, because Brother André was my great-great-uncle." Peppe pointed to himself and added, "Yes."

"You're kidding!" I exclaimed. "The only reason I know about Brother André is because he's the great-great-uncle of my friend Denice! You and my great friend are...fourth cousins!" This only mildly amused him, but I grabbed my phone, called Denice, and left her an excited, garbled message about Brother André. *Your cousin—Peppe. Oh, I'm in Montreal. Call me!* When she did call back a few days later, her nonchalance made me question my exuberance. Was it the excitement of traveling so footloose to a new city? Or how much I love the topic of saints? Or, dang, was the glass of wine just a little too big....

Kateri Tekakwitha was born into the Turtle clan of the Mohawk, one of the six Iroquois nations, in present-day upstate New York. Her mother, an Algonquin, had been raised in the Jesuit mission of St. Francis Xavier du Sault outside Montreal, but during one of the frequent warring periods, she'd been captured by Mohawks and brought to live among them, to marry and have a family. Thus Kateri's father was a Mohawk non-Christian and her mother an Algonquin Christian, although she was forbidden to practice the religion. As she lay dying, Kateri's mother whispered to her little girl about the love of Jesus, whispered that she should pray to the one God.

When Kateri was twelve, Jesuit missionaries, or

"Black Robes," arrived to visit the chief. She was put in charge of caring for the guests because her vision problems meant she wasn't much good in the fields. These missionary-guests brought back the words of her mother, and Kateri was drawn to them. They told her how Jesus had suffered to bring the light of God for all people, everywhere, not just the lucky few. The missionaries did not stay long in Kateri's village but left her with basic instruction and prayers. Her ability to memorize amazed them. In general, Native Americans' memorizing skill for the smallest detail of landscape for a hundred miles in any direction, without a map, was mind-boggling to Europeans. Can you imagine saying, "And yes, once you've gone up the coast for two days, you will see a ravine where the eucalyptus grow. A boulder beyond there is where the fresh water is." (Or the wine-tasting room.)

For several years, Kateri prayed those prayers and sought to learn what she could about Christianity from others who were quietly practicing. At nineteen, her clan moved to the north banks of the Mohawk River, near what is today the town of Fonda, New York. A Jesuit, Father Lamberville, was in charge of the nearby St. Peter's Mission, and it was to him that Kateri went in search of baptism.

Well, Bill finally arrived in Montreal, several hours late, after those beautiful storm clouds I'd watched from the train forced his plane to land in Syracuse to wait for the weather to clear. This is just the kind of thing that cements his belief that travel's for the birds. Waiting on the tarmac, hideous. The line for a cab, a nightmare. The rain.... I listened sympathetically, nodding at the right moments. After thirty-three years of marriage, I know to just give him a chance to come around. After a good night's sleep, off we went, searching Montreal's old quarter for croissants and café au lait. By old Montreal, I don't mean like Old Town Pasadena, where we live in California, which means 1930. Here "old" means 1630. The cobblestones and high granite steps that take you into little shops with jingling brass doorbells are so fun. Everywhere, people are speaking French, everyone bundling up against the cold breezes blowing through the trees. All just a five-hour flight from LA. We did find them, the perfect croissant and coffee, in a warm, French-feeling café. And after that, we found a Lyft.

St. Kateri's shrine was a half-hour ride without traffic. Moustafa, in his mid-sixties, picked us up in a gleaming Honda Accord and we were off, across the St. Lawrence River to tribal lands. You always know where a Lyft will take you, but a modern pleasure is never knowing where the conversation will go. Moustafa was telling us about the Algerian War of Independence from 1954 to 1962. He said that every Friday, from then all the way to now, Algerians strike and demonstrate. "It makes life completely unstable!" Moustafa announced, throwing his hands off the steering wheel in frustration at the traffic. Montreal's freeway system was torn up and seemingly under total reconstruction, but finally we left behind the skyscrapers and congestion. Moustafa continued, "I had to get to a country where I could find success."

Crossing the river, I gazed at the amazing St. Lawrence. It carries water 500 miles from the Great Lakes to the Atlantic Ocean. It's full of bass, pike, perch, and—you'll be amazed—closer to sea, almost a dozen types of whales! We were nearing the town of Kahnawaka, the town where Kateri's shrine is located. There are so many pronunciations for Kateri Tekakwitha! Just break it down to *Tek-a-kuee-ta* or *De-ga-kuee-ta.*

Even though light hurt her eyes, Kateri was highly skilled in the traditional arts: bark baskets, canoes, burden straps, beadwork, and embroidery. But her kin grew increasingly hostile to her. Sometimes they threw stones at her or denied her food if she wouldn't work on Sunday. Kateri spent more and more time away from others, preferring to be solitary, to pray as she worked, to sit in the deepest quiet of the forests. Gentleness, simplicity, and purity were her hallmarks, noticed and remarked upon by Father Lamberville and other priests.

Father Pierre Cholonec, her spiritual adviser, wrote an account of her life in 1685, available in paperback today. (Once again, I was reading a text with language so thick with age, it took some M&Ms to get through it.) Father Cholonec said that Kateri tacked a cross to a tree, and there, in summer and snow, she would kneel. In the abundant forest outside her settlement, Kateri proclaimed, "This is my place of worship." Nature, the greatness of the outdoors, is perhaps for all of us our authentic place of worship. Where can we better sense wonder? There is a forest of camellias at the world-famous Huntington Gardens, near my house. To walk among those towering shrubs, their tips heavy with blooms hanging just out of reach, is a wonder. Not always, not if I'm in a hurry. But with attentiveness, the geometry of the blooms, the range of the colors, and the huge amount of time they take to grow are God in the everyday to me.

Kateri is a patron saint of the environment. Her attunement to the seasons, the moon, the harvest—what berries and fungi to eat, when to fish—all of it was a deep part of her mysticism. She was of a people whose depth of knowledge of the natural world is inconceivable today. Fire, wind, rain—these elements actually dictated her day. So different from what shapes the days when I work at a computer. There are berries in the hedge, though, just out my window, that I gaze at to rest my eyes.

When it came time for Kateri to marry, things got heated. Girls simply had to marry. The alternative was unheard of. Who would protect you? Who would keep poverty away? Besides, your clan surely needed another hunter to add to its strength. Did she want to be a weight on everyone in her old age? There was no way out. It was then that Kateri knew she must run away and live in the mission if she were to dedicate herself solely to God. She waited for her chance, and when it came, she made her way 200 miles north on foot and, with assistance, by canoe to the mission of St. Francis Xavier du Solut, where her mother had grown up. There she was greeted by acquaintances and distant family members who'd also decided to live among the

Christians. She never returned to her clan's settlement.

We were nearly there. I realized I'd zoned out of the conversation Moustafa and Bill were still carrying on. It's so easy for my mind to wander delightfully out the window, but it's also the reason it took me six years to finish college.

We passed a "Welcome to Kahnawaka, Mohawk Reservation" sign and followed more signs through town that pointed us to Kateri's shrine, built on the original site of the mission. No more longhouses or traditional village life. No forests nearby. Today there are tidy, wide streets, cheap gas, tobacco stores, and modest little houses built here, there, and everywhere. Quiet people getting by.

At the mission, Kateri had freedom to practice her faith. She lived in deepening devotion to God. It was said that every breath she took was of and for God. One of the great traits of the Iroquois was testing themselves for courage, strength, and fortitude, and especially for the ability to withstand physical pain. Their survival and honor depended on these attributes. Kateri translated this into forms of extreme penance or mortification. Father Cholonec described her rolling on hot coals, breaking the ice and plunging herself into freezing water, kneeling in the snow for extended periods, even wearing thorns. Earlier I mentioned where I stand on this, but in learning about Kateri, this aspect of her devotion comes up again and again. In these states of pain, she felt she could transcend herself and be very much closer to God. When the mission fathers discovered the extent of her mortifications, they insisted that she curtail them. She obeyed, but there's surmise that these practices broke her health. After a painful decline, Kateri died at just twenty-four.

Her very short life. What does it mean? How, exactly, does this add up to sainthood?

As Kateri was dying, her last words to her friends were, "I will love you in heaven. I will pray for you. I will assist you." And at the moment of her death, mystical events began occurring. Those tending her witnessed how the scarring on her face suddenly vanished. A wonderful perfume wafted from her. Her entire being became beautiful. Those in the hut, including Father Cholonec, became afraid and ran away. But they came back and stood in astonishment. Her body stayed like this for many, many days, and people from all around came to witness it, even the ranking priests from Montreal and Quebec City. According to the Jesuit diaries, the priest could not be heard at her funeral due to the cries and sobs of those in despair at their loss.

Six days after Kateri's death, Father Claude Chauchetière, another mentor to her, had the first of many visions from Kateri. She prophesied a coming war among the French and the storm that would destroy their church. She foretold the martyrdom of some of her kinsmen, and through her intercession, miracles started to happen. It is said that benefits have flowed from her life from the moment of her death up to the present, and that she is a powerful intercessor for those seeking physical healing.

There's a social movement called Kateri Circles. For the past eighty years, Kateri Circles have formed on almost every Native American and Canadian First People's reservation, as well as in many archdioceses across both countries. People pray and ask for help with all their daily challenges. The group's intention is to welcome back Native Americans who have felt mistreated by the faith. Kateri Circles celebrate cultures and bring tribes and families together, either at special Masses or at powwows.

Back home, I had had the pleasure of attending a Kateri Circle Mass at a parish southeast of downtown LA. Members took part in drumming and sage burning, the sage held aloft in abalone shells fitted with elk-horn handles. With hawk-feather fans, two men waved the scent up into the air. The congregation joined in the prayer of the four directions: east, north, south, west. There was a prayer to the saint. And then Mass continued as usual. Afterward, about fifty people gathered for the potluck: an array of meat dishes, salads, macaroni, cakes, fruit, Coca-Cola, and coffee.

Being alone, I ended up sitting with a warm and inviting woman named Connie, of the Yaqui tribe, who lives in Claremont, just a little east of LA. The Yaqui are one of the twenty-seven tribes of Southern California. Beautiful, with fun eyeglasses and well-styled silver hair, Connie surprised me by saying she was seventy-seven. "But you look so young!" I blurted. "It's my Native blood," she said with a wink and a laugh. She still worked as a community outreach specialist for child development programs.

"What do you think Kateri's message is today?" I asked her.

"Forgiveness," Connie said without hesitation. "She was treated horribly by her own people, and she forgave them everything. They stoned and shunned her because she was different. It was harsh back then. They threatened her with real torture, but she ran away before that." Connie paused. I listened for her next words. "You cannot move on, you cannot develop spiritually, until you learn how to forgive. Her mother died when she was little, and her stepmother and father treated her terribly. She rose above it. She could not be a holy person if she couldn't forgive." I nodded in understanding.

"Is Kateri your main saint that you rely on?" I asked.

"Well, the Virgin Mary is first—I think of her as my own personal Jewish mama. Very helpful, very directive, very wanting to know what's going on. But then, yes, Kateri. These two forces helped me very much when my son died."

"Oh..." I murmured.

"Died of an overdose. He was a druggie. But I never, never stopped loving him. I showed up for him always, always—nineteen years in prison. Ask me anything you want to know about any prison—I know it." She waved her hand in certainty. Stoic in emotion. After a moment, we both smiled, because life goes on.

What does it mean to ask a saint for help? It is not praying to them; it is asking for them to intercede for you. A saint, whose energetic capabilities are strong even after death, can help our wants and needs be heard by the great love of the universe.

So you can pray through St. Anthony when your keys are lost. Or St. Valentine for love. Or St. Kateri when you are sick. We often need someone on our side, to get our voice heard, when dealing with a higher authority. A lawyer helps us navigate legal matters. Nancy, real, live Amtrak Nancy, assisted me with a ticket. Many people have a special devotion to a particular saint and look upon that saint as their special helper in emotional and spiritual matters.

We said goodbye to Moustafa and stood in front of a solid, gray-stone church. The only actual image we have of Kateri was painted by Father Chauchetière, who was inspired by his visions to take up a paintbrush shortly after she died. A banner with a depiction of that painting hung from the spire of this church, her shrine. We opened the little chain-link gate and stepped over damp, lumpy grass to a walkway. It seemed like everything was all closed up. But then people popped out from a side door, and we realized the shrine was open.

The warm aroma of incense and the sound of soft Gregorian chants greeted us as we entered. A jewel of a frescoed interior, all from 1720, and no one there but Bill and me. It was so beautiful and so, so far away from life in California. We loved the plaster statuary and altar silver, the paintings of the Virgin Mary, the solitude. And then, in a side chapel to the right of the altar, we saw a massive, rectangular, Carrera marble tomb, completely unadorned except for gold lettering across its face: KATERI TEKAKWITHA.

I noticed again how powerful it is to sit—just to be—before the tomb of a saint. It's like staring at a sunset or a starry sky. Not much—actually nothing—is happening. You are just wonderfully there. A little basket to the side held pencils and paper. I knelt down and prayed out a note to her: *"Dear Kateri, keep me well. Keep me free of negativity. Keep my family together in solid affection for one another. Help the whole world fall in love with nature again, our natural earthly world, the world our lives depend on totally and completely. Keep technology within limits, so some things remain ever simple. Protect me."* I folded the note and put it in a little slot. I lit a candle. Bill was in the back, doing his own private thinking. After a bit, creaking floorboards made me turn around. Two older ladies had emerged from the gift shop.

"Hello," I said, approaching them. "I'm Mary Lea Carroll. I'm the one who called you several times from California. I made it! We got here! Is one of you Sandra?"

"That's me," said the one with thick white hair and blue eyes. "This is Diane; we work together. Would you like to see the museum?"

They took us back to what used to be general rooms for the Jesuit missionaries and were now housing displays of vestments, utensils, and prayer books. There hung Father Chauchetière's painting of Kateri. Wow. It's the only original image we have of her, but it's been copied everywhere, even on the cover of the paperback book I had on my desk. It was not behind glass. Suddenly I remembered my younger brother Kevin and me, in 1973, standing in front of the *Mona Lisa*—no bulletproof glass, no ropes, no sensors, not even any people on that long-ago day. Kevin whispered, "I want to touch it, I just do," and then he moved closer. "I'm going to!"

I turned sharply and hit him across the shoulder. "Don't you dare!" I pushed him away. We both started laughing. Ugh! We were so stupid when we were young.

The gift shop was hardly more than an arrangement of Kateri rosaries and prayer cards, vials of holy oil, and a small selection of books. I looked everything over.

"Were you born here?" I asked Sandra.

"No," she said with a smile. "I'm from Scotland. I married a native, though. Lived here a long, long time."

"And Diane, are you from here?" She nodded quietly. She had short, grayish-brown hair in a bob, eyeglasses, and she wore a powder blue mock turtleneck sweater. "Are you native?"

"Oh yes," she said simply. "I'm from here."

Maybe they could give me insight. I asked, "Ladies, how do you reckon the history of Indian schools? Weren't they harsh on the culture? And to some of the children? And often run by missionaries?" I also wanted to know how the Church saw this today. After all, according to the flyer on the shrine's bulletin board, the church was participating that week in Orange Shirt Day for "those who survived Indian schools and those who did not."

The question seemed too big for the moment. The

women looked to each another, two old friends. They shrugged. Looked a little into space and tried to answer, but just...an answer didn't come. They were not evading it—it was more that the question seemed to tire them. So instead, Diane asked, "Would you like to see the relic?"

"Yes, very much."

She went away and came back in a few minutes carrying a box wrapped in a piece of cloth. She took the cloth away to reveal that the top of the box was glass. Lying within, on gold fabric, was a four-inch piece of Kateri's bone, edged with delicate gold braid and encircled with small pearls and sapphires. The little piece of bone curved. It looked almost like wood.

"Oh...can I touch the glass?" They both nodded and smiled proudly.

"Father keeps it covered and away, except for groups. But you've come from so far," Diane said. I put my hands on the box, half hoping for a jolt of electricity or kaleidoscopic prisms or—something. But I settled for smiles from them, just as they got smiles from me.

I did buy a few little things from the shop, and then I had to ask, "Diane and Sandra, does anybody ever come out here?"

"It's almost winter. In the summer we get busloads, even from Europe!" Sandra answered with pride. "We will need to restock before then."

I made a final stop at Kateri's tomb, bolstered with energy from seeing her relic. For a moment, I laid my head on the cool stone. I know this sounds silly, but I was trying to be as open to mental and spiritual benefits as possible; taking all the help I could get for my aging brain to...you know, not go batty.

And then it was time to head back. Our phones didn't show a Lyft or an Uber anywhere nearby. We asked Diane and Sandra if they knew anyone whom we could pay to take us back to Montreal. They made a few calls. Pretty soon, a gray mom-van pulled up with a giant guy at the wheel. We settled on $40 and set off with Willie.

Willie said he was doing everything he could to make a few more bucks before leaving the country on Friday. He was a performer, a Mohawk rapper, and he and his band were headed to France for their "Wake Up the World" tour. His first time to France. "Gotta wake this world *up*!" he announced. "Complacency's gotta change! We've got to learn to love the land again! The environment! Before it's too late. Politics gotta change. We're going to go over there and *blow people's minds*! We go the whole indigenous route. Dress, everything."

I was smiling ear to ear as he sped us along the far side of the river, soon to cross back into the crazy traffic, not of 1650 Ville-Marie but of 2019 Montreal. Thank you, God, for such variety in life! When Willie dropped us off, Bill turned to me and said, "Geez, that guy never stopped talking!" Again, thank you, God, for the variety in life.

Prayer to St. Kateri

Like the bright shining stars at night, we pray that your light shine down upon us, giving us hope, peace, and serenity in our darkest moments.

Holy Doors

While warming up over a bowl of soup in Quebec, we listened intently to our new friend, a tour guide named Jacques. "You know, of course, about the British conquest. So don't miss Artillery Park. And the Plains of Abraham; probably you've been there already, yes?" He read our blank stares. We shook our heads. He scolded us lightly: "Didn't you study *anything* about Canada before you arrived?" Then he added, "And, of course, you realize you are so close to the Holy Door, yes?" Bill and I shot each other a glance.

"Yes," we lied in unison. I wanted to be writing all this down on my hand, under the table so Jacques wouldn't know how ignorant we were. Battle sites, okay, whatever; I'm really not that interested. But Holy Doors? That's something to know about. And actually, yes, yes, it was coming back to me. When Pope Francis declared 2015-16 a Year of Mercy, the *Los Angeles Times* ran a piece on Holy Doors in the travel section. Friends of ours actually ran off to Rome expressly to step through the Vatican's Holy Door. They weren't even Catholics; they just loved the idea that cities around the world were opening their Holy Doors. For the Year of Mercy, every archdiocese in the world devised a Holy Door, but only eight are perpetual.

Amazingly, one of those eight in the whole world was just 500 feet away from where we were having split pea soup. Pope Francis granted Quebec the privilege of creating a Holy Door in the Cathedral of Notre Dame, which sits so beautifully in Quebec's old town. The cathedral especially, but all of old Quebec, is a UNESCO World Heritage Site. It is the only fortified city in North America. You can wonderfully lose yourself in the 1640s by wandering the streets and lanes and alleys within the walled fortifications.

Holy Doors come from an idea started in the 1300s, but they actually have far more ancient roots.

The Greeks, the Egyptians, and even cultures further back shared the idea of symbolic passages through portals to…what? A new land, a personal achievement, a cleansing. These Holy Doors offer a crossing-through for a new you, or for shedding sadness or disappointment. Some people use them to mark a new phase of renewal. Some step through one on a honeymoon. One can step through from sin to grace. They are open to all people of good will and of all faiths.

Holy Doors can be created only by a pope. Four times a century, the church calls a Jubilee Year, and that's when the doors are opened. Catholics might decide to take a pilgrimage to a city with a Holy Door to step through it. Rich blessings can come from this. As it is said, "Ask and you will receive; seek and you will find; knock and the door will be opened to you." Some call it a symbolic ritual of reconciliation with, say, a neighbor, or an event, or with God; restoring in yourself things that have been damaged.

The rector at the cathedral put it another way: *to step from the outside to the inside as if we were trying to enter our own self. We are looking for the meaning of our future, to quest for sense in our lives and in our world.*

"As if we were trying to enter our own self." To straighten out the threads of our hopes and counterproductive habits, our obligations, and our deep desires… these threads get so tangled up over the years. If a journey to simply walk through a door specially created for one's deepest personal quest was available, who wouldn't want to go? Oh, the whole idea is marvelous.

Bill could go on to Artillery Park. I walked right

over to Notre Dame and its vast and magnificent interior. Gilt ornamentation swirled out and up above the altar. Two thousand people could easily kneel and say prayers in here, but on this Wednesday afternoon, it was all clusters of tourists listening to tour guides. Between the side chapels, naves, and niches, it was impossible to tell where the Holy Door might be. I approached a group of well-dressed ladies who seemed to be studying the stained glass. They would know. "Excuse me, is one of you a tour guide? Can you point me toward the Holy Door?"

"The what?" answered the one with dark, curly hair. She had a rich Southern accent.

"Oh, sorry. I was told there is a Holy Door here."

"We're just a girls' trip havin' fun from Texas," said another, causing us all to laugh. Fun! I wanted to be on a girls' trip from Texas.

"But we'd like to see something called a Holy Door, too," said the one with dark hair, named Barb. We introduced ourselves, and then we were all on the same egg hunt. These four gals and I spread out, looking, looking. We poked into every part of the oldest church in Canada. Then one of the women came running back to me and exclaimed, "We found it! It's over there, on the west wall of the big side chapel!" I hurried after the band of Texas gals. And there, quietly huge and hugely impressive, was a bronze door cut with two severe slits in its middle, forming a cross. The cross let shafts of light in through the heavy metal. A luxurious red ribbon tied the door shut, its knot protected behind plexiglass. Holy Doors may only be opened every twenty-five years, so the next time they open, around the world, will be 2025, unless the pope calls an emergency, like he did in 2015-16 for that Year of Mercy. He ordered all the doors opened. Pope Francis felt the world needed an injection of mercy—*now*!

"Wow," we seemed to all say together.

"Wow," I said again as I had my turn to go up and touch it. A Holy Door. Who knew this day would give me the chance to actually know and experience this? Of course, it was closed—but I was good with just standing next to it.

Barb and the Texas girls, friends from high school, kidded with one another the way friends do as we took turns clicking photos of each other at the door. I got their whole story. Barb was the "ringleader." She'd inherited a ring from an elderly aunt and decided to auction it off at Sotheby's. Well, it brought more money than her wildest dreams could imagine! In the spirit of *You only live once*, she gathered her girlfriends together, and in celebration of her good fortune, took them on this trip, paying for everything. They were on a "pray, pubs, purchasing" getaway: visiting churches to pray and pubs to celebrate. And get this: Barb had given each friend a couple thousand dollars for shopping, but with a caveat. The money had to be spent on gifts for others. Spread the good fortune. Well, I just fell in love with them.

"Mary Lea, come with us," Barb said. "We're going to go find Irish coffee somewhere." Her friends also urged me to join them. I looked at my watch.

"Well, sure!" I wanted to say. Why not settle in

with generous Barb and her besties and chase away the cold temperatures and the innate loneliness of life? That's what friendships do. Laughter, a warm pub, and a hot Irish coffee mean just one thing—a good time! I so wanted to head with them into the beautiful, cold October air, but I didn't. Bill would be wondering where I was. So we said our goodbyes. They went their way, and I went mine.

Eight permanent Holy Doors exist in the world: four in Rome, one in Santiago de Compestella, one in Formans, France, one in Manila, and the one here in Quebec. Even though this door was closed, seeing it made me glad. It feels mysterious, this potent spiritual ritual. Come 2025, I want to be at one of those doors when it's opened. That's five years from the time that I'm writing these words. Where possibly could I be in five years? That would put me beyond seventy. What I want is to be five years further on a never-ending journey of self-discovery, keeping as my compass the saying *It's not the destination but the journey*. It makes me think of the Teresa of Avila quote that I love so much: "The road to heaven *is* heaven."

Three

A Mystic in the Classroom

St. Marie of the Incarnation
1599-1672
Quebec, New France

Bill and I had just finished an early morning walking tour of Quebec, a city that sits so picturesquely on the banks of the St. Lawrence River. Four hundred years of history whisper and wink through winding alleys and wondrously old architecture. Now, Bill wanted to peel off and chill in our small Hôtel du Vieux. Actually, chill isn't the right word—we were freezing in the fall temperatures of the Great North. He wanted a warm room and a football game. After we parted ways, I looked around and found that I was standing in front of the stone Chapel of the Ursulines and its 350-year-old elementary school. Five steps away was the contemporary Ursuline museum. I didn't know anything about the Ursulines, so I thought, *Hey!* And went in.

Turns out, Quebec simply would not have become

Quebec without them. They were the first female missionaries and the first order of nuns to arrive in the New World north of Mexico City. The French had claimed the territory all the way from Newfoundland to Louisiana for themselves. Just to remind their competitors who got here first, they named all of it *New* France! Never mind all the First Peoples, the tribes of the Iroquois League and others who'd been on this land for 13,000 years. Britain got it away from the French in 1763. As for the United States, we would get our part in 1803 with the Louisiana Purchase. But for almost 200 years it was all New France.

A tiny band of hardy ladies—and by tiny, I mean four in number—is recognized as founding the first school for girls and anchoring the Catholic faith in all of Canada. Jesuits had been there for thirty years already, but there'd been no female presence until the four Ursulines landed, in the company of a Jesuit priest and two Augustinian nursing sisters. The year, 1635. The leader of the Ursulines was Marie Guyart, a thirty-six-year-old woman from Tours who adopted the name Marie of the Incarnation when she took religious vows.

The vast wilderness and the indigenous peoples who lived there tested the courage of Marie and her bunch. She had left France at its zenith of culture. Europe had been "civilizing" itself for 1,500 years by that time—you know, cutting down its forests, eradicating wild animals, and codifying behaviors (acceptable forms of torture, for example). But the territories of New France? When Marie arrived, Quebec was just a name on a riverbank. There were five houses.

I remember the courage it took when I too discovered a new land. The stakes weren't *quite* as high, because I was at Disneyland. But I was only five when
I ventured all the way to Tom Sawyer's Island on my
own. (My brother Jeff was *supposed* to be watching
me.) I took a little faux-real raft across the faux-real
river. By myself. What a wild place it was! Any wild
thing might jump out. And I lived!

Marie's path to the wilderness and to her love for
God began when she was a small child. According to
her diaries, she had her first mystical experience at age
six, when she looked into the sky and saw Jesus hov-
ering in the air. As He moved toward her, she became
enveloped with an overwhelmingly wonderful feeling.
She found herself reaching her arms out to Him, and
He reached out to her. Jesus asked her, "Do you want
to be mine?" She called out, "Yes!" From then on, she
was, in her words, "inclined to goodness." By fourteen,
she had asked to enter religious life. But her father insisted that she marry a man he knew, Claude Martin,
a master silk worker.

By her own account, Marie enjoyed a happy marriage, brief though it was. Within five years, she was
widowed and left with a tiny son. Now, at nineteen,
she inherited her husband's business, but it was on the
brink of bankruptcy. Marie figured out how to allay the
creditors, get rid of the debt, and sell it off. For the next
several years she and her little son, Claude, lived with
her sister's family and helped manage their household.

Here, her business skills blossomed. She began
helping them run their busy transportation business,

sometimes working sixteen-hour days. She wrote, "I would spend entire days in a stable which served as a store; and, sometimes, I was on the wharf at midnight, directing the loading and unloading of goods. My usual company was that of dockers, carters, and even fifty to sixty horses that needed tending."

Throughout all this intense activity, however, nothing distracted her. "I was constantly occupied by my intense concentration on God," she wrote. When she read Teresa of Avila's autobiography, *Vida*, written fifty years earlier, she was struck and deeply moved by Teresa's mystical experiences and recognized her own depth of experiences. Marie's mind was literally always on Jesus—trying to keep deeply connected to Him, no matter what else she was doing. *Vida* became her aid as she moved toward a contemplative life.

Entering the little museum, I found it to be filled with all the items necessary to teach boarding students in 1650 and later—strict little mathematical books, narrow beds and nightstands, arcane science equipment. The handsomely framed embroidery samples were so gruelingly complex that I could imagine all the tears spent in trying to achieve such precision. Only the butterfly and bug collections gave me pleasure. I'm so glad I wasn't asked to be successful in such an environment. All of this looked like torture.

Although, to be honest, school *was* torture for me, and Kevin, and Dan, and John—we're the ones who flunked, all in one fell swoop. One day Mom just pointed to each of us and said, "You, you, you, and you—you're all going back a grade." Come Monday morning, instead of being a fourth grader, I was back in third grade again. It was particularly confusing for Kevin, though. He'd skipped first grade, sank in second grade, and, like all of us, had spent two months already in the next grade before flunking back. So Kevin did second grade two times—but went on to skip eighth grade, when he changed schools, then had to do ninth grade twice! He would not touch college with a ten-foot pole. As adults, my sister Sally and I surmised that it must have been menopause that caused Mom to lose it so badly over our report cards.

Classrooms like the one on display here at the Ursuline museum were the very best New France and many other places had to offer back then: a boarding school, taught by nuns. And for those girls who could hack it, the sisters did indeed give their students training, status, and manners that helped them succeed in New France. What will people 350 years from now find torture-like when they look back on schoolrooms of today?

I stepped out into the cold, breezy air. Shoot, it was only October—how cold does it get in Canada? I headed across the way to the Chapel of the Ursulines. That day it was so quiet inside. The beautiful cream and gold walls and warm woods made me think of antique French jewelry. I took a seat in the back, enjoying the sense of history and loving how warm and well heated the chapel was. Wait—really, how *did* the missionaries deal with the cold? I was wearing a down jacket, and it was definitely not enough! How did Marie and

her band survive the Canadian winters in stone houses? One account says that these frontier sisters slept in
chests modeled after coffins so they wouldn't freeze to
death. That's a fun idea!

Why did they venture so far from the known? The
kingdom of France in the seventeenth century was a
positively cushy place compared with this. Here, the
missionaries ran the risk of being captured by Mohawks who'd been horribly treated by foreigners. In
fact, not long before Marie arrived, one of the chap-
lains of Quebec had been captured, tortured, and then,
well, devoured. Of all the bad things that could happen
to you in France at that time, that one was just, you
know, not on the menu. But Marie was determined to
spend her life here. Hardship, not a problem. In fact, it
was an opportunity to perfect herself—to strengthen
her capacity to rely on God.

Let's go back to Old France for a moment. When
Marie was finally able to enter the convent, her son
was twelve. She left him in the care of her sister's family
and dove into a cloistered, contemplative life, unteth-
ered from the workaday world. In dreams that were
full of conversations with God, He told her to move
"quickly, quickly, do not delay," and she understood
this to mean come to the New World. But everyone
thought this was a terrible idea. Her mother superior
said it was too lofty for a woman to want to enter the
man's world of missionary life. Her spiritual director
said she was too physically and spiritually weak. Her
brother threatened to cut off her inheritance. So she'd
have to find the money to make it happen.

Marie then met a wealthy aristocrat, Madeleine de la Peltrie, who was totally on her side. Madeleine also had a huge spiritual calling and was in want of an adventure. But Madeleine's family—why is it always the *family*?—would not allow her to use her funds in such an outrageous manner. So she did something outrageous: She entered into a marriage of convenience in order to gain control of her money. As a married woman, she could use her inheritance as she wished. With no further ado, Marie of the Incarnation, Madeleine de la Peltrie, and the two other Ursuline sisters set sail on the *St. Joseph*, a small, three-masted galleon. These four were the people who would found the first school. Also on board were two Augustinian nuns, who created the first hospital in New France.

It took three months to sail the 4,400 miles in the *St. Joseph*. The voyage seemed like one hellish episode after the next. One storm lasted fifteen days, and unless they held tight, they all rolled about the floor in great sickness. Another time the women were put into a much tinier room with the stores of fish. The heat was worse than a bread oven. The smell was finally beyond standing. They went up on deck to sit, though the rain poured down day and night. They lived on a kind of stale pancake. Once they came so close to an iceberg that a sailor started screaming, "We're dead! We're dead!" Through the dense fog, they just missed it. When they arrived in Quebec, the governor and his lieutenant were at the shore to welcome them. Later, one of Marie's sisters wrote about how hard it was to be so dirty in the company of those so honorable.

Once Marie had her feet under her, she set about her business. Many natives of the Huron tribe were allies of the French, so Marie quickly had both Huron and French colonial girls to teach. First, the Ursulines had a wooden house in which to live and teach. Within a few years, with Madeleine de la Peltrie at her side, Marie oversaw construction of a larger, stronger monastery up on the plateau in the high town. Young women attracted to teaching and living in a community were coming to her. So were students.

From the back pew, I scanned for where Marie's tomb might be. There it was, to the side, huge, black granite, surrounded by red-padded kneelers. In gold letters, "Marie of the Incarnation." I made my way over there and knelt, letting myself be free for whatever thoughts floated in. What is it like to "empty yourself for the will of God"? Marie continually strove for this.

Words from Mother Teresa of Calcutta floated to mind: *Jesus will use you to accomplish great things on the condition you believe much more in His love than in your weakness.* Maybe that's what Marie of the Incarnation did. In the face of fear and hardship, relied on God to fill in for her weaknesses. Maybe that's how everybody does it: Rely on a power bigger than yourself, as my AA friends say.

Kneeling there, I said *Thank you.* Thank you, Marie of the Incarnation, for being a model of boldness, toughness, and determination. I want to face what my life offers with boldness, too.

Well, the monastery was nowhere near out of debt when, in the middle of a freezing night in 1651, it burned down. One of the sisters had forgotten to extinguish the embers under the bread bin that kept the dough from freezing. The sisters and students barely escaped with their lives! Marie was able to throw all the important papers out the window, saving them before herself. But then there they all were, maybe twenty of them, standing barefoot in the snow. The Augustinian nursing sisters took them in. Everyone expected the Ursulines, and Marie in particular, to throw up their hands in defeat and head back to France. After all, they were now homeless and up to their eyeballs in debt.

But no! As soon as the snow melted, Marie began rebuilding, this time in stone. She knew financial support could only come once ships sailed back to France, related their woes, and then made the return. On faith—that hardship is all part of God's plan, and our job is to stand up to it—she negotiated with workers, borrowed from Peter to pay Paul, did whatever she could to keep going. The parents of students came with aid. And for those who witnessed it—her planning, her overseeing, even climbing the scaffolding to work on the building herself—the swift construction of the new monastery was called miraculous.

Marie used her evenings to study and write by candlelight. (So much is possible if you don't have Netflix.) She and her sisters learned the languages of the surrounding tribes: Huron, Mohawk, Algonquin.

Following the Jesuit example, they created dictionaries and sacred texts for them. Today, amazingly, indigenous peoples wishing to revitalize their languages refer back to these early dictionaries, as they are the only written records. Over her thirty-seven years on the frontier, Marie wrote tens of thousands of letters back to friends, supporters, and her son—a historian's gold mine of accounts of life in New France.

August 24, 1658:

> *The Iroquois have gone back on their word and broken the peace.* [The French were not excellent at this either.] *They had even conspired to kill all the Fathers and all the French who were with them, but the Lord took them by the hand and protected them.... There is still another reason I spoke to you about last year, namely the losses that our Lord has permitted to befall us. Two days before our harvests a great whirlwind accompanied by a crack of thunder flattened the barn of our little farm, killed our oxen, and crushed our plowman in an instant. Two days ago, yet another calamity befell us. The Iroquois called from afar to a young man grazing our oxen by the one little house remaining there. Intending to capture him, as they had a cowherd several days earlier, he ran away. When he composed himself and returned, the house was aflame. The five oxen, gone. Next day, we found the oxen in quite a distance. Terrified, they had dragged a long piece of wood which was attached to them. One was dead. The house was of little value, but the loss of furniture, arms, tools, and all the equipment causes major inconvenience. It is thus His Goodness visits us from time to time.*

Marie's letters also brim with her mystical experiences, which the harsh wilderness sharpened: the hunger, the fog, the heat, the loneliness.... Suffering through these trials was a gift, she said, that allowed her to strengthen herself and her bond to the source of all strength, Jesus. She earned the names Mystic of the New World and St. Teresa of Avila of Canada. She wrote that her relationship with Jesus was beyond language, an inexpressible sensation that might start in traditional prayer but quickly deconstructed into breathing in and out simple phrases, like *love, love, Jesus, love, love, love*.... She could remain in a state like that for long bouts of time. However, she also learned how to harmonize contemplation with worldly activity.

I stepped outside the chapel to look through the chain-link fence into the bouncing, active schoolyard of the Ecole Ursuline, founded in 1639—and still in full swing on the spot Marie built it! Amazingly, the contents of the little museum had come directly from this school. Boys began attending in 2012. It looks like an elementary school anywhere. Teachers with walkie-talkies or coffee cups in their hands. Backpacks tossed on the steps. Ruckus and play in the asphalt yard.

Later, back at home, I had the opportunity to be "principal for a day" at Altadena Elementary School, until recently one of the lowest-performing schools in the Pasadena district and, coincidently, where I went to kindergarten. I hadn't stepped foot on the premises since I was five but remember acutely that on the first day of school, Mom had dearly promised she'd be right there waiting for me when I got out. "Don't be scared—I will be waiting right here!" Well, she wasn't. I was standing there, the last one to be picked up, and by then I was crying. She arrived in a big hurry, holding or hanging on to my four younger brothers and sisters. My little five-year-old heart felt so betrayed, and there was no excuse that would console me.

But oh, what can happen when a school decides it will become the best! The library looked like the Barnes & Noble children's section. The theater room, the dance studio, the art stations at recess...I loved it all. This recently strife-torn school teaches French, starting in kindergarten. That just seemed plain excessive. But when a kid in the fifth grade greeted me *in French*—well, I was literally envious. Oh, for a do-over! I was born too early for modern education.

Marie followed a deep calling to teach the love of Jesus Christ to students she felt desperately needed it. And in her mind, indigenous girls had to become French girls—in language, dress, and domestic arts. It was their only path to success. This was culture clash at its most dramatic. But French culture did take deep root in Quebec. To this day, everyone speaks French. More than eighty percent of Quebeçois are Catholic, maybe not churchgoing, but still Catholic. It's a patriotic thing, in that the Catholic French did not like taking orders from the Protestant British, not then and not now. Point in case: the recent conversation, yet again, for Quebec to break from Canada so it can be its own place. Quebec really celebrates that the city was founded by saints; their statues are everywhere.

So, who *was* St. Ursula, from whom the Ursulines took their name? She was a princess in fourth-century Roman-ruled Britain, pledged to be married to the pagan governor Conan Meriadoc in Brittany. She declared that before her marriage, she'd take a big pan-European pilgrimage, basically a grand-scale bachelorette party. She gathered a group of like-minded virgins, some say as few as eleven while others say as many as 11,000. (Hang on, this is legend.) They sailed to Rome under a miraculously safe wind, had a wonderful time, and carried on with their travels overland. Unwisely, they took a scenic route home, up through Germany. While stopped in Cologne, they were besieged by Huns—all of them getting slaughtered on the spot. That just ruined everything.

If you go to the Basilica of St. Ursula in Cologne, you'll see a veritable tapestry of patterned bones, floor to ceiling. So, so many human bones, and all of them are supposed to belong to those virgins of St. Ursula's bachelorette party. (One account does say, however, that they discovered a few mastodon bones in the mix.) Before you throw the baby out with the bathwater, disbelieving all of it, know that there is a Roman cemetery for the martyred beneath the site of this basilica. We have to forgive time for its exaggerations. Though St. Ursula is clothed in legend, she and her maidens, be they eleven or 11,000, stand for virgins martyred everywhere. Thus, it made sense when, in 1535, the

Italian noblewoman Angela Merci named her new order of nuns the Ursulines, because their purpose was the education and defense of girls. Belief in St. Ursula, regardless of her verifiability, created something real.

In 2017, after 380 years, the Ursuline sisters of Quebec moved from the monastery to more comfortable accommodations for their aging population. When the evening news asked Sister Helen, herself advancing in age, how she felt about leaving their historic home, she said, "Of course we hate to go, but if Marie could leave France and everything she knew behind, we can, too." The reporter asked what motivated her to become an Ursuline at age twenty. "Ask any sister and you get the same answer: It was a desire to be with Christ above all else."

That is a good answer but also hard for me to understand. As a woman, I definitely wanted marriage and motherhood. But I'm full of admiration for Marie of the Incarnation—she went out into the wilderness so boldly. She personifies a good metaphor, for isn't each of our futures an unknown wilderness? She turned fear of the unknown into a chance to rely more heavily on God. She feared nothing.

The saints speak across time to one another and to us. Marie of the Incarnation, with all her setbacks, seemed to say this to me, but it was Hildegard of Bingen who said it to us all:

> *"Even in a world that's being shipwrecked, remain brave and strong."*

Marty

In north Pasadena and Altadena, my small corner of the LA megalopolis up by the mountains, so many people know Marty, the guy with the white hair and the silver truck. They consider him a friend. People use the same few establishments in Altadena's tiny business district and run into one another often. Marty says hi to everyone. He's got a flexible work schedule. You'll see him at the supermarket, you'll see him at the hardware store, you'll see him at the bike shop with customers and the owner, Steve, discussing bicycle mechanics. Marty makes the time for that five-minute chat on the fly. Lots of us do not—not because we're unfriendly but because we're preoccupied or in a hurry. Too often we forget how important these micro-encounters are in maintaining a sense of belonging and geniality. Marty keeps this small civility alive.

Marty is up for helping anybody with practically anything, and he's got that thing we all need at times: a truck. Need to move a bed set? No problem. Need to barbecue for a few hundred? No problem. When our kids were in elementary school, this came up often. A neighbor's toaster has broken? Bring it over, no problem. Want to know how a power washer works? How to restore a camper? How to fix a leak? Marty not only knows how, but he lets you know you are not bothering him. Sometimes he gets hired to help out, but more often than not, he just does it to be neighborly.

Bill and I were in the midst of a coyote invasion.

They'd skulk around the bushes, popping out in broad daylight from behind the garage. When we found them sitting on our patio chairs like they owned the place, Bill flapped his arms, yelled, and banged pot lids together. Finally we said, "We gotta talk to Marty!" Soon he was sitting at our kitchen table. "We're at our wits' end," I cried.

"They're everywhere," Bill added.

"They're so brazen!" I continued.

Marty nodded in agreement. "Bill, you'll love this," he began. "What I do, and it's working, is you have to urinate on the areas the coyotes are claiming. Human male urine." Our faces scrunched up. "Weird, I know, but for some reason it seems to work."

"What an assignment!" Bill said. We laughed about the details of this desperate measure, and then talk turned to all kinds of other stuff. I realized how seldom I have a really long conversation with someone, because usually my mind starts darting around with other pressing concerns. But Marty's generosity with his time has a calming effect.

"Marty, do you ever get bugged that everyone asks you to help them out because you have a truck?" I asked.

"Oh yeah," he said, chuckling. "That's part of having a truck. I don't mind. If I can help someone out, I like it." Why doesn't Marty mind being imposed upon? When we needed help with our coyote problem, he came right on over. Why help so many people move stuff? Why does he make it his business if a neighbor's appliance breaks?

"The thing is, I really like people. It's usually interesting. And fun." He shrugged. "It's not a big deal. And there are people out there who haven't got anyone to talk to. Maybe I'm the only person who's said hi that day. Some people are almost shocked when a stranger says hi—'What? What did you say?' I laugh and say, 'I'm just saying hello.' And after a while, we become friendly."

Our local market hires special-needs people to bag groceries. Shoppers are patient with them, but I've seen Marty standing still in the parking lot long enough to really talk with Mikey or Jason. To find out what life is like for them.

Marty will just knock on someone's front door if he's curious about something. For instance, he loves old campers. "If I see one down a driveway, I'll knock on the door to talk to the person about his camper," he said. "I've made a lot of camper-friends from doing that. It's just knocking on someone's door, to be friendly. Why do people think that's so out there?"

As we sat at the kitchen table, I basked in his positivity. Marty reminds me that we are indeed our brother's keeper. Doing favors for one another is the way of tending the net that holds us safe. What Marty does is pretty simple but not that common.

Footnote: The coyotes have stopped coming by.

Four

Over the River and through the Woods

GOOD ST. ANNE
50 BC–12 AD
Canada

No matter how mystifying the Virgin Mary's biology was, the fact is she had to have had a mother. Jesus had to have had a grandmother! Good St. Anne lived so long ago, and her story really has no facts attached to it. But she is named as Anna for the first time in the year 150 AD in a gospel attributed to St. James. In Islam she is called Hannah, saying, "God has favored me with a child." The first known image of St. Anne in the west appeared in the Byzantine frescoes of Santa Maria Antiqua church in Rome, in about the eighth century.

What *do* we know about her? Well, we know she was real, that she *had to have* been alive. And that she did a righteous good job as a mother. And as a grandmother. You don't get a child like the Virgin Mary if you haven't done a good job. What qualities would she

have had to have? Unending patience, a calm and generous mind, wise counsel, the ability to gently teach....
I say gently because, gosh, haven't we all had harsh teachers from whom we learned nothing?

Anne is the patron saint of dozens of cities around the world in Spain, Italy, El Salvador, France, and more. She's the patron saint of Quebec. Quite naturally, she's the patron saint of grandmothers and mothers, plus teachers, sailors, and, *phew*—protection in storms! She's been depicted by the Renaissance masters, including da Vinci, Rubens, and El Greco.

And I wanted to see her bona fide forearm, which has to be 2,000 years old. It's housed in the Basilica Shrine of St. Anne de Beaupré, outside Quebec City.

I'd traveled to Montreal to learn more about St. Kateri. Little did I know that saints dot practically every corner of Canada! On the pro side of traveling ignorantly, there are so many surprises. On the con side, you can miss what's right in front of you. Thankfully our guide, Jacques, clued us in. He was as fit as the hockey player he'd once been, as patient as the ski instructor he was currently, as smart as the Jesuits who educated him, and as knowledgeable as the baker he was on the weekends. "You absolutely, one hundred percent, must take the drive out there. You will be amazed, I promise you. One hundred percent!" he said as we chatted at a coffee stop on our walking tour. It was Jacques who'd insisted that we find the Holy Door. He also recommended the wine from the vineyards east of the city. I wrote down his tip to taste "Seyval blanc."

So the next day, Bill and I rented a car and drove

north through the splendor of autumn along the St. Lawrence River. To give Bill a car, a map, and a destination is his idea of heaven. Coming from Southern California, it all felt so far, far north. Fields and farms and forests as beautiful as a children's picture book. We were literally going over the river and through the woods to grandmother's house—to the town of St. Anne de Beaupré (meaning beautiful field). The largest and oldest North American pilgrimage site for a saint, it started when sailors in the early 1600s were trapped in a storm on the river and prayed frantically for St. Anne to save them. And they were saved! So then and there, they built a chapel in thanksgiving, and thus began what we have today. It's a Gothic-style basilica that easily takes up a city block. Seating for 1,500. Half-ton bells that ring from the spires, a thirty-foot water feature, arrays of saints and angels created by master stone carvers, and endlessly beautiful mosaics and stained glass. Plus everything needed to accommodate hundreds of thousands of visitors a year. It sits prominently amid the small town of Beaupré.

We entered quietly. A funeral was in progress. We reverently tiptoed through a group of tourists craning their necks at the high altar and ceiling. I headed straight to my destination: the Great Relic, the golden-gloved arm of the sainted grandmother. I could easily see her arm bone through the fashioned opening of the gold glove. It looked like polished wood, in its crystal and gold display case, or reliquary, as it sat high on an altar in its chapel. Bill started looking down at his watch.

And then there was the statue of St. Anne herself, atop a twelve-foot pink onyx pillar. It's a miraculous statue, with healings attributed to prayers said before it throughout the centuries. Golden rays shot out all around her, and hands reached out to beckon us. "Um, honey, I'm going back to the car. I've got a book," said Bill, and he headed for the exit. I kinda knew the 2,000-year-old arm wouldn't hold him.

Tilting my head up, I saw a mesmerizing mosaic of four angels on the high ceiling, spreading St. Anne's cape out wide to protect and heal those who come to pray and ask for their ailments to be alleviated. And indeed, there is a wall of canes and crutches back by the entrance.

I'll happily take any benefit from prayers offered before this beloved relic of St. Anne, the exemplar of goodness. The, the...*grandmother* of Jesus. My mind began conjuring. Would Anne and her husband, Joachim, have gotten a bumper sticker for the family van: *Our grandson—he's the greatest!* or *Our daughter—she's number one!*

Bill and I had been pretty happy to stick—permanently, grrrr—a bumper sticker proclaiming: "Grace Happens" because our middle daughter, Grace, seemed more like a person who "happened" into this world rather than one who arrived in the normal way. Here's an example from when she was little. She started a hobby at lunchtime of collecting everybody's tinfoil and rolling it into a ball. Pretty soon all her school friends were helping. The ball got bigger and bigger. The day she brought it home to show me, it was the size of a big footstool. She said, "Mom, it's my pet. His name is Rin Tin Tin." We'd seen that bumper sticker on a car in a parking lot and then saw the couple, just leaving. Bill and I called out, "Hey, love your bumper sticker!" and surprisingly they reached into a box of them and gave us one. It's the only bumper sticker we've ever had.

The arm bone I stared at was given to the shrine by Pope John XXIII, who brought it here in 1960 as a gift to the people of Canada. There's a photo from 1980, when John Paul II visited, of him prostrating himself before the miraculous statue. St. Anne's arm bone had been in the care of the Vatican since 1333. Before that it had been in St. Sophia's, in Constantinople, since 707, when it was brought from the Holy Land. Or it might have been discovered deep in a chamber of the Cathedral of Apt in France. The mists of time leave questions—small details that can get muddled in a very big picture.

What would I want to pray to St. Anne for? I knelt down. How about ever more strength and the desire to do and be more? And for my own motherhood, even though my daughters are grown up. Help me be what's needed now; help me to offer good advice and to keep my mouth shut. Help me to both be there and not be in their way. I prayed for possibly being a grandmother—to be a magical, fun, fairy grandmother. A grandmother who'll bring out a box of treasures, who'll take them on trains, who'll have the patience for loud noise, who won't be too tired.

I kept my head down. What would it have been like to have a child like Mary—perfect-in-every-way

Mary? My own mother, God bless my own Good St. Jane, wouldn't have known, even though she had nine tries at perfection. But she knew perfection when she saw it—it was in the family across the street. We could see their house from our kitchen sink. They had almost a dozen kids, too, but those kids got good grades. They were not late for church on Sunday morning; we knew, because we always saw them leave ten minutes before us. Those teenagers didn't burn the flag or defy authority like Jeff and Sally. Or crash the cars like Danny, Jim, and Jeff. Or get arrested like Jeff and Dan and me—me, ridiculously, for parking tickets! None of the boys across the street wanted to wear their mom's nail polish, like Kevin. All that, okay, Mom could live with that. But when she saw their oldest son drive up and hop out of his clean, un-dented VW with a bouquet of flowers—well, Mom slammed her hand on the kitchen counter, whipped around, and shouted at us, "You damn bunch a kids!" Who knew it was Mother's Day? Dad was working out of town. I'd like to think it wasn't the big deal it is today, but the kids across the street somehow knew it was Mother's Day.

No, St. Anne would have known how to instill better behavior in her children—she just would have. But then, my dear mom was the daughter of a pie-in-the-sky Irish alcoholic and a silent-movie star who, into her eighties, survived on her looks and her indignation.

Thank you, I continued, as I prayed for my long-gone parents, Jane and Jack. They did the very best they could. How could they, born in the 1920s, be equipped to raise so many children in the 1960s? Neither one of them knew what "peace and love" was all about, much less rock 'n' roll. They knew the Depression. They knew Frank Sinatra and cocktails. They knew never having enough money. We pushed 'em pretty hard, for sure.

One night when I was about seventeen, I saw my dad outside, pacing the front porch. I asked, "Dad, is everything all right?"

"Oh, honey," he sighed. He sat in a folding lawn chair and flicked his cigarette away. "It's just too much." Instantly I regretted going outside. Whatever "too much" was, it scared me. I quickly found a reason to head back inside. Shortly after, Dad finally did find work, but 2,000 miles away. It was a huge relief to my parents, as he'd been looking for almost a year. But Mom was left alone with five teenagers, two little ones, and two in community college—well, let me tell you, it was *par-tay* on Santa Rosa Street.

When Jesus was growing up, when money problems came, I'm sure the family would have worked together and stayed close. Jesus would have known if his dad was embarking on the loneliest, most miserable stretch of his life.

Help me, Good St. Anne, to be the person God has in mind for me to be. Banish baseless thoughts like the fear of getting old. Fear of breast cancer. Fear of...stop! The Bible repeats "Be not afraid" 366 times. Once for every day of the year, and once again for—leap year? Actually, this *was* leap year! That's fun, perfect timing for an extra dose of Be Not Afraid. St. Anne, your shrine has stood on this spot for 350 years. Let me partake of the peace, generosity, and wisdom of who you were.

When my mother, Good St. Jane, was sick and dying, she started talking about her childhood. How, during the Roaring '20s in New York City, she'd have to put her hands over her ears when her parents fought. One time her dad, the flamboyant Jim Cassidy, came home and announced he'd bought a flower shop in the lobby of a grand hotel in Florida. They were all moving ASAP. This was during a Florida land craze. It was all set. My grandmother Ruthie was to be the florist. She screamed at him, "What do I know about flowers? There goes all our money!" But they went. Things were okay—till the hurricane hit. All that was left of the entire hotel was the over-the-moon-expensive walk-in refrigerator for the flowers. So, back they went to New York, and back to Jim Cassidy's favorite bars.

For years, Anne and Joachim remained childless. The high priests told them they must be sinners or God would have granted them a family. They tried harder to be good. Still no children. In olden days, and by that I mean all eras except the present, people wanted and needed children. Children meant prosperity, signs of great blessings, and—bonus—free help in the restaurant! Or whatever the workplace was. It's not that people don't want children today, but it's now often a choice, not an intrinsic, inescapable, wholly expected part of life. After twenty years, Anne, in a dream, was told that their deepest desire would be granted, and a baby girl came to them.

Tradition suggests that Mary was born in Jerusalem. The church of St. Anne sits on that spot, and millions visit the thousand-year-old church that's next to the miraculous pool of Bethesda. With astonishing acoustics, the church draws musicians and vocalists from around the world. Someday I'd like to be able to go to the Holy Land and see the place myself.

And to have a grandmother like St. Anne? She'd have offered you her lap. She'd have had a voice that made you happy. She'd have been soft, would've known how to play with you. It's good to have role models. My mom's mother, Ruthie—*Don't call me Grandma; Grandma makes me feel old*—would sit in our kitchen and watch Mom cook dinner for twelve as she sipped her five o'clock gimlet. She'd cross her legs and swing her high-heeled foot. Click her loose dentures, sip away, make helpful comments to her exhausted daughter. "Jane, dear, why don't you wear a girdle? Jane, dear, Kevin's not very masculine, is he? Jane, dear, get Jeff to cut that godawful hair." Mom would just keep peeling potatoes and ripping open big bags of frozen peas.

St. Anne would have helped with the cooking. Grandma St. Anne would have babysat for Joseph and Mary when they went out. Well, to be fair, Ruthie did teach us how to read the racing forms and how to get your money back if you didn't like the shoes you'd already worn. I asked God to bless my long-gone Ruthie for doing the very best she could. She had to quit school in the third grade to go to work, cleaning houses. Because of her beauty, at age fourteen she won the title Queen of the Coney Island Mardi Gras of 1912. That launched her in silent movies. But when everything went south in the stock market crash of '29, she began her life as a saleslady, selling shoes, dresses, and, finally, newspaper advertising. She did that for decades and decades. But the beauty-queen movie star in her didn't leave much room for helping out around the house or with her grandkids.

Good St. Anne, protector in storms. There's a phrase I rely on quite a bit: *I am protected in the storm of change.* It helps me when fear, or attempting the audacious, puts me into a kind of personal storm. If *I know I am protected, I know I am safe,* then I know I will come through. When we turn to St. Anne's qualities while we're in meditation—wisdom, patience, generosity, the careful education of our children—those very thoughts are in fact generating *wisdom, patience, generosity, the careful education of our children.* Because even just thoughts have the power to create.

Good St. Anne, since I do my best to never get into a boat, I doubt I'll be in need of protection from a storm at sea—but for the storms of life, please throw me a rope.

When I stand before God at the end of my life,
I would hope that I would not have a single bit
of talent left, and could say, "I used everything
you gave me."
Erma Bombeck

Bonnie

The mother of our friend Michael is the sweetest little old lady you could ever hope to know. Bonnie's in her high eighties and still cooks up a storm. She loves and remembers everyone—that is to say, all of us. Michael's circle of friends out here in California. She wants to see us and hear everybody's news when she visits from Florida. Bonnie's always got a note of laughter in her voice. The two things that amaze people about Bonnie is how much joy for life she's got, and how determined to live she was when she was young. Bonnie was the only member of her family to survive the Holocaust.

From the age of nine to fourteen, she hid in the woods, hid in barns, hid in attics. First it was her mother and father and brother with her, hiding from the Germans. None of them survived, and then it was just her, a skinny preteen girl who learned to handle what she calls one fear at a time; don't look at the whole picture—every situation is temporary. If she had to learn quickly how to milk a cow, she learned quickly. She begged door to door, would disappear to reappear in another town, sometimes wearing a cross, sometimes not, sometimes speaking Russian, sometimes speaking Polish. She learned to sum up a person or situation in an instant—will they turn me in, or can I get food from them? She cannot recall one instance of kindness toward her. Everybody had a motive: Pretend you belong to us, that way they won't take all our bread. Or, want to hide in our barn? Okay, but take this money and deliver it at night across town. Or, you look cold. Want this coat? Okay, but stand by this gate and tell us if anyone is coming. And that's what she did, on her own, for three years, after her father and then later her mother and brother were caught. The Nazis missed her because she'd had the wherewithal to hide under a mattress in a corner of their attic hideout the night they were caught. When the war ended, she landed in a children's relocation camp. For the year she was there, she learned English and how to sew. One day, officials came through and said, *You have to choose. Want to go to America or Israel?* Bonnie's mother, Ann Frankel-Hoffman, had a cousin in the United States, and she had made Bonnie memorize the name Leo Frankel, New Jersey. So at age fifteen, Bonnie arrived in the United States. She soon found herself a sophomore in a normal American high school. She lasted two months in that "ridiculous place" and quickly found work on 5th Avenue in Manhattan, altering high-end women's clothing. All seventy-plus years ago.

"Bonnie, you don't seem bitter at all. Why is that?" I asked as we sat together at Michael's and his wife, Suzanne's, house. We each had a cup of tea. Her hands were folded before her. She looked at me keenly.

"I am grateful. I made it. Life is a wonderful thing, and I've had the chance to live it. How could I waste life on not being glad I survived! In those days it was always in my mind, 'I've got a future, I've got a future, I've got a future.' And when I realized the war was over, what I did was go after my future." Today, in her old age, Bonnie stays busy speaking to groups and schoolchildren about this period of time and her childhood.

I sat back, grateful myself to be with her in this moment that seemed outside of time. Her conviction! Her wits! Her personal power! Bonnie did not call it that; she called it instinct. Okay, instinct, yes, but it was more than that. It was bravery, fearlessness, smarts, an indefatigable desire to squeeze every bit of living out of the life she'd been given. I got to sit across the table from this tiny, four-foot, ten-inch force of nature, wondering how I would measure up if I'd been in her shoes.

Five

One Disabled Woman's Power

MARY VIRGINIA MERRICK
1866–1955
Washington, DC

"Let's go have some fun!" That's what I said to Brigid when I invited her to come with me to DC. Washington was the first stop on my trip east, before going to Philadelphia. I wanted Brigid's help and her company in handing out copies of *Saint Everywhere* to representatives of the National Christ Child Society at their annual convention. I'm just a rank-and-file member, and I was excited to be there. They're a great bunch of women. In fact, for the past 133 years, women in this service organization have been volunteering for the betterment of children all across the country. And super interesting to me, Mary Virginia Merrick, the founder, is on step two toward sainthood! Mary began with just a needle and thread, sewing for one poor family. That became an army of laywomen "finding a need and filling it."

Washington, DC, back in the 1880s and '90s, had swollen with pockets of great poverty. For years after the Civil War, all types of unaided destitution prevailed: lame veterans, street urchins, widows (*lots* of widows), freed slaves, and new immigrants with nothing. They filled tenements that became known as slums or alleys. The Italian immigrants were the builders of the big government buildings and the iconic Union Station. Relief services for these groups were almost nonexistent.

Mary's mother would take her along on visits to poor families from a young age. Mary read the novels of Charles Dickens as a teen, and her family was prayerful—these things helped warm her heart to serving those in need. Her mother also took her on trips to a lace-and-needle shop to buy supplies for their home sewing. Mary got to know Miss Delarue, the shop owner, who was supporting her aged mother and a few other families in need through the shop's meager profits. Mary asked if she could sew a few things for some families. Thus, with this small act, she began a life of doing all she could to alleviate poverty, especially among children.

When Mary was sixteen, she fell from an upper window and was paralyzed. She spent the rest of her life in a lay-back wicker wheelchair, enduring constant pain. I asked my doctor, Stephen Henry, how do people actually endure constant, chronic pain? He sighed. "Well, at a certain point you just have to take your mind off it. For your own sake, you have to force yourself to keep living your life and moving forward." Mary did not despair and instead doubled down into her prayer life. And her active and organized mind would not let her feel sorry for herself. Her sisters and her friends rallied around her. Her home became a hub of coming and going as Mary continued her efforts to sew clothing for needy children.

She learned of a baby, to be born at Christmas, whose mother had so little that the baby was to be wrapped in newspaper. She organized everyone to sew for this baby. They made such a clean, beautiful lay-ette that the mother was emotionally overcome. This was so inspiring to Mary that she reached out and got even more friends to join her. In 1884, when she was twenty-one, Mary formed the Christ Child Society— named because she could see the divine baby in the face of each poor child. The gifts she made or acquired to put a little sunshine into a neglected child's Christ-mas would always be signed *from the Christ Child*, as in, *You are noticed and you matter to God*. She'd spend the rest of her long life building this organization.

Mary was only twenty-one, and she was disabled and in continual pain. This just gets me pondering: Why did I let so much time get by when I was in my twenties, cocktail waitressing in that country-western fish house or, for months, lying in the sun on a Greek is-land? I mean, none of it was wrong, but did I not know that time is finite? Could I not have attempted more?

Today, there are forty-four chapters across the country, with 6,000 volunteers carrying out Mary Merrick's vision. Some chapters work with hospitals and homeless shelters, low-income schools and literacy centers. Some work directly with principals of Catholic schools, alleviating a family's tuition crisis. All are extending the work of a woman who is on her way to sainthood.

"Somehow saints" are everywhere: people living large and small heroically good lives, but who are unknown outside their circle of friends and family. To be one of those who somehow make it to the big time—full Roman Catholic canonization, with your own holy cards and a feast day—a somehow saint needs several things. Primarily, a strong group of people, living, who are so moved by your life that they champion your cause. You can't do this for yourself because, of course, you're dead. Mother Teresa of Calcutta was canonized swiftly. It only took six years. For many saints, it takes hundreds of years. Many incredible people are on the road to sainthood but never make it all the way. In the end, it is the pope who makes the decision.

From the hotel where the Christ Child convention was, all fifty of the chapter representatives boarded a comfy motor coach to take a little tour of Mary Virginia Merrick's life. Brigid nudged me as we took our seats. She knows I love bus tours—I was once a pretty great bus tour guide myself. After I saw, at eleven, that underrecognized genius of a film *Gidget Goes to Rome*, where *she's* a tour guide, I wanted to be one, too. Have you been to San Francisco and taken a Gray Line city tour? That was me. It's great fun to view a city from up high, through the window of a bus. We weren't in the monument or touristy part of DC, though. Our route took us through the neighborhoods of Chevy Chase.

We pulled up to the cemetery. Statuary of weeping maidens draped over headstones set the mood for a good graveside visit. Elms created a restful verdancy, and rustic footpaths wended us up hill and down dale to Miss Mary's headstone. We all stood in a loose semicircle around it. It was just so simple, so unassuming, like the countless Christmas letters Mary's group received. "I never had a doll," wrote a little girl. "I want a big doll as I have TB and no-one will sleep with me." "Please, I want a nightgown." "My father needs his shoes now. He found work. I want shoes."

Within a few years of its founding, Christ Child began offering fresh-air programs and summer camps. Then their tutoring, books, religious instruction, and lantern-slide presentations on cultural topics spread to jails, TB clinics, boys' homes, and settlement houses for immigrants. Mary learned how to attract all types of social groups to her cause to build her ranks. All the while she was at home, on a couch or in her wheelchair, surrounded by ever-larger groups of volunteers. The wives of every US president, from Harrison to Truman, either donated to or wrote about Mary Virginia Merrick as her organization grew. President Harrison's wife had donations delivered on horseback. It spread to other cities. Eleanor Roosevelt wrote columns about her.

As we stood gazing at Mary's tombstone, a handsome older woman named Patty Myler stepped forward. She asked us to join in the prayer for Merrick's canonization. And so we began. What a completely unique experience this was, to actually participate in an effort to have someone canonized. We all know saints through the stories or their big shrines, but this is how it starts, before there is a shrine or anything, really, other than the lasting quality of their good deeds. The beginnings of canonization: people praying for you, and Brigid and I were partaking in this exalted process. Patty had been busy compiling the history and details of Mary's life for the archdiocese of DC. They opened the application for canonization in 2003.

As we hopped back on the motor coach for a visit to Mary's home, Patty took the mic. "One of Mary Virginia Merrick's quotes that we can all relate to is:

> *And if by accident, I cannot accomplish the work that I set for myself on that particular day, I should not let that disturb me as that only comes from pride.*

I could see the chapter presidents nodding their heads. I know of no other social service organization in this country dedicated to child welfare as old as this, fueled by volunteer laywomen (not nuns). It has weathered two world wars, the Great Depression, and women's liberation from traditional roles. Like, how many women today have *time* to join a service group? They barely have time for their own kids. But new chapters continue to be formed as the condition of children in this country continues to be woeful. Woeful. Los Angeles County alone has 30,000 children in foster care. Half of them will end up on the street when they "age out." Mary Virginia Merrick was considered a groundbreaker in the new area of academic study called "social work" and the emergence of organizations labeled "nonprofit."

Her street and home look like they were lifted straight off the set of *The Music Man*—white picket fences, brick sidewalks, tidy nineteenth-century yards. We trouped up the wide wooden steps and were welcomed in. "When we bought the house fourteen years ago, nobody told us it was Mary Virginia Merrick's," said Bridget Overcash, the gracious owner. "I had no idea, and I'd been a member of Christ Child in Atlanta before moving here. Please look around, everyone, and help yourselves to lunch." Neat box lunches were stacked on the buffet. Yes, we saw photos and memorabilia of how the society grew exponentially, from providing a few dozen gifts at Christmas, some layettes to newborns, and shoes at Easter to tens of thousands of these items annually, plus scholarships and reading programs. But, okay, what amazed me was simply standing in Mary's house, so very much like any historic house in my hometown of Pasadena. You think of a saint's quarters as austere or secluded, but this home should be on the cover of *Southern Living*, with its stylish, sherbet-colored rooms. It made me very happy to have Mary's life look so...relatable. We think of holy people as, well, *too holy*, people too holy to have coffee with, but this lovely home felt so human and full of comfort.

The last stop of the day was exciting for me: her *thrift shop*! For eight-five years it has been a major support for the DC chapter—in recent history, generating millions of dollars annually. Generations of Washington's elite women have donated their finer things—paintings, handbags, scarves, you name it—knowing that one hundred percent goes to Christ Child works. In the 1920s, Mary's growing band of helpers held weekly rummage sales, not so much to earn money but, in the spirit of assisting those who had almost nothing, preserving the self-respect of the buyers. If a man asked how much that hat was, the lady would say, *Well, how much were you thinking?* If he said a dollar, she'd act surprised and say, *Oh, I was thinking—75 cents.* Today, this surely is the granddaddy of all charity thrift shops. I got some pearls. Brigid found a perfect yellow scarf. The two-story shop was buzzing with all of us finding good buys. Wonderful to me that one of the enduring aspects of a someday-somehow saint is a thrift shop. How my mother and sisters would've loved it.

Back in the '60s, Mom would go off to the market to get food for dinner with a "Be back shortly" but actually return several hours later and with a U-Haul behind her. There'd be surfboards, maybe a leather trunk, and who knows what all else. An antique hair dryer? She'd discovered a brand-new thing called the yard sale. "Can you believe it? All these things were just spread out on the grass!" She was a pioneer in the yard-sale movement. Then she'd have to hide all this stuff from Dad. My mother loved breaking rank from the rigors of being a good Catholic mother to us nine children. Treasure hunting at yard sales was her kind of fun. Of course, no matter what mind-boggling finds were in that U-Haul, the question remained, "But

Mom, what's for dinner?" She'd say, "My gosh! Here, one of you come with me. I have to return the U-Haul, then we'll see about dinner."

My older sister Sally took yard sales far beyond me or Bethie or even our mother. She made her second career at it, sifting through other people's things as an estate dealer. God broke the mold when He made Sally. She had a lot of rules for her business, one being, "I won't do an estate for *anyone* if they are alive." Through the cigarette perched between her lips, she'd say, "It's too sad for them to get rid of Aunt Gertie's rocking chair. After I've already cleaned it, polished it, and priced it," she'd throw up her hands, "they carry it back inside. No, my clients have to be dead or I won't work with them." Another of her rules? "No collecting empty boxes. Do you even know how many old ladies' closets are stuffed with empty boxes from defunct department stores?"

My wonderful, slightly cracked big sister died three years ago from brain cancer. Sally had two good years after her diagnosis, though. During that time, she said a remarkable thing to me: "I pity people who die instantly."

"What?" I said. "You've got to be kidding."

"No, I'm not. I never would have known how kind people could be if I'd died instantly." Wow. You go, Sally.

So many layettes, so many babies. What exactly *is* a layette, you may ask? The term comes from the old

French, meaning a box or a chest. Traditionally, a mother would hand-sew beautiful clothing and bedding for her coming baby while pregnant. Into a Christ Child layette go all the necessities for a good start: sleepers, tiny T-shirts, diapers, lotions for mom, a baby book, and always one item made by hand. That could be a blanket or maybe a cap and booties. Knitters and crocheters all over the country help with this. It's a small sign that someone cares about you and your new baby, even though they don't know you. These layettes go to all types of agencies that find the mothers in need. Of course, a mother in poverty will need far more than a layette. But it is a clean and hopeful beginning. It's like giving that baby a kiss when, perhaps, few others will. Mary Virginia Merrick lit a lamp and said to her friends, *Let's do this!*

The kingdom of Heaven is like a mustard
seed which is indeed the smallest of all seeds;
but when it is grown, it becomes a tree and the birds
of the air come and nest in its branches.
Matthew 13:31-32

Jesse

At first I was afraid of Jesse. He looked like the strongest bodybuilder in the world, and I'd just signed up for unlimited workouts with him at his new gym, which was full of heavy cross-training equipment and reverberated with rock 'n' roll. Nothing like my former holistic, lady-wellness routine that finished with aromatherapy. Jesse's clients left big, frightful drops of sweat all over the place. But his gym was really close to home, and my other fitness person had closed her business. Plus, the first week was free. By the start of the second week, I was comfortable in the back and worked out at my own speed. Jesse took us through our paces in the most patient way. Each person he worked with got his best attention, even someone like me, twenty years older and twenty pounds heavier than everyone else.

One day I noticed Jesse's tattoo. Right up the middle of the inside of his arm were the words *Follow Your Bliss* in large, fanciful script.

I looked at it for the next several weeks. When the time was right, I said, "Jesse, that tattoo must have a story." He smiled and nodded. "Tell me what it is," I asked. And the two of us took a break and sat on the bench press. He got out his phone.

"You're new," he reminded himself aloud. He smiled his nice smile. "I got this twelve years ago when I finally quit the job I was making so much money in." He pulled up a picture on his phone. "I'd had that job for, like, ten years. And this is me at my high school graduation." Jesse, the strongest man in the world, was gigantically obese in his graduation cap and gown.

"No way!" I exclaimed.

"Oh yeah, 340 pounds. And I'm not that tall. But a light went on that day. I realized I'd done this and I could undo it. And I did! It took a few years, but I got super into fitness and nutrition. I lost all the extra weight. I didn't go to college, I tried it, but no. But I'd learned to take care of my health. I got that great job I mentioned, with Fry's Electronics. Remember them? They're out of business now, but twenty years ago, they were everywhere. I was a manager, working my way up, all this money coming in, everything was great. But I didn't like it at all, and I was too afraid to quit.

"When I was twenty-five, my roommate's dad said to both of us that we should watch this series on tape called *The Power of Myth*, with Joseph Campbell. We sat around and watched every episode. Then I re-watched it. To this day, it's on Audible for me, and I'll listen again to bits and pieces of it. It blew my mind! So much changed for me when I understood the things he was saying. Joseph Campbell coined it—*Follow your bliss*." Jesse held his arm out again for me to see.

"Up until I quit the good job, I'd never done what I really, really wanted to in life. And what I wanted to do was this!" He looked around his gym. "Help people feel better. Help people achieve their fitness goals. I was too afraid to go out on my own and start a business. By taking to heart this teaching—*Follow your bliss and the universe will open doors for you where there were only walls before*—I found a way to actually do what I knew deep down I was supposed to be doing. This concept is so important to me that I wanted to always be reminded of it." Jesse's eyebrows danced up and down as he smiled. He stood up and went back to helping a client with some weights.

Joseph Campbell says he came to this idea of bliss from the Upanishads, ancient Hindu sacred writings. Campbell wrote, "There are three terms that represent the brink, the jumping-off place to the ocean of transcendence: Sat-Chit-Ananda. The word 'Sat' means *being*. 'Chit' means *consciousness*. 'Ananda' means *bliss* or *rapture*."

You don't always know who exactly you are, what exactly your consciousness is, but you know rapture or bliss when you feel it. If we hang on to that, we find our true path. "Following my bliss"—whatever that meant—was practically impossible for me when younger. What hung me up was this question: If I strove to be, or somehow got, all that I really wanted, did that mean others would then somehow have to get less? Was it selfish to want the moon? I didn't know there was, in fact, enough moon for everyone.

Six

Making Good on a Promise

Mary Lea, let me rent the car, Brigid said. "That way I can try out something bigger. I'm so tired of a little car." I'm happy to let others drive. We had an extra day in DC, and it turned out that Emmitsburg, Maryland, wasn't that far. She went off to get a car.

Before long, Brigid reappeared, driving a ridiculously big black SUV with tinted windows. "It's the only bigger car they had!" she lamented.

"It's what rock stars ride in," I said, laughing. And like rock stars, off we went to find St. Elizabeth Ann Seton's shrine in Emmitsburg. Brigid's niece Keely, a brand-new teacher in one of DC's poorest schools, was navigating. We'd kidnapped her to spend the night with us in a nice hotel. Poor thing, working long hours and taking the bus an hour each way to her classroom.

Me, I just rode in back like a VIP, staring out the blackened windows, giggling at the silliness of us in this car.

Brigid, what a lifelong friend! Our moms had been college chums, we'd been travel buddies for so many trips in our young twenties, and she is godmother to my girls. The Irish have a term, *anam cara*, soul friend, and that she is. We hadn't gone anywhere together in a long time, not since the Amazon and Machu Picchu four years ago.

Ye gads, what a trip! I'd caught a fungus that grew and grew all across my face and hand. The dampness of the jungle acted like a steroid for it. So we had to get an emergency flight back to Cusco and a doctor, but lordy, the doctor didn't seem older than fifteen. She sent me right to the hospital. Brigid sat in a chair next to me all night long in that unnerving place, which seemed more like a loading dock than a medical center. Next day, pumped full of harsh antibiotics, I was good to go. How we laughed at such crazy misfortune back in the lobby of our Cusco hotel, as we imbibed the complimentary oxygen and plotted the next part of our trip.

St. Seton's beautiful shrine came into view after an hour's drive, VIP style, through the scruffy harvested fields of Maryland. Do that many people want to visit St. Elizabeth Ann Seton? See her body? I mean, I do. But that's because I'd visited her small, almost unnoticeable shrine in Manhattan and had written about her in *Saint Everywhere*. I'd promised myself back then that if ever I were to get the chance to check out her big shrine, I would.

What courage she had! A woman who seemingly had it all: society status as a good Episcopalian, a dashing husband, five children, and a big house in Manhattan, where she entertained people like Alexander Hamilton. But then, at the age of twenty-nine, she lost her husband and got stranded, penniless, in Italy, where they'd gone to try to rescue his health. Once she found her way back to New York, she lost her social standing. She took in her late husband's much, much younger brothers and sisters. Oh, gosh, a few of her own children died. But then she came to a great personal awakening through a new discovery: the Catholic faith. It was this that helped her blaze a groundbreaking life.

We swung wide into the parking lot of the minor basilica and museum complex. Gardens all around gave over to the surrounding farmland, all quite beautiful. There are still about sixty acres left of the Fleming Farm, as it was known when Ann Seton moved here in 1809. From here she founded the first American order of nuns, the Daughters of Charity. Here, she started her free school for girls. We each paid the eight-dollar entrance fee and signed on with Richard, soft-spoken and amiable.

Richard strolled us across the field to a tiny Colonial-era structure called the Stone House. He explained that Seton and fifteen other women shared this space, nothing more than a hearth room and two tiny, crooked rooms off to the side. A ladder went up to a loft, which apparently let snow in on the sleepers. One big iron hook in the hearth to hold the pot for cooking.

Period. Nothing more. How could they have managed? But these privations must have looked pretty good, because growing numbers of young women arrived to join in Ann Seton's work.

We strolled across to what they called the White House, built a year later. Oh good, they only had to live in the tiny Stone House for a year. They had to create space for even more young women, who continued to join the order. The sisters and boarding students lived upstairs in the White House. Downstairs...oh, wow, what a classroom! It was set the way Ann Seton actually had it arranged. Ten little chairs. Ten slates. A concertina. A grandfather clock. And a chalkboard displaying perfect—I mean perfect—penmanship, like only the nuns could do. Ann Seton's desk held a crock of writing quills. Everything was just so stringent and exacting. No colors, no stickers, no shiny, playful books. Just the simple supplies for one adult to instruct ten children with an air of authority and rigor. Almost inconceivable in today's world. I could see Keely's mind working. Her hyperactive little second graders would eat this room alive. Her classroom is full of corkboards and art and colorful alphabet letters running along the walls.

We were standing in the very classroom from which all parochial schools sprang. St. Seton reminds me of Mrs. Fields and her cookies, a chocolate-chip cookie empire that began in one kitchen and now has franchises in almost every major city. Could St. Seton ever have imagined her school system going global, as it did?

What struck me as I toured the downstairs rooms

was how austere their lives were. Just in my own kitch-en alone, I have at least ten different appliances for cooking, and that doesn't include the stove. Can you imagine all your clothing having to be spun? Not in a factory somewhere, but spun by you! Then woven by you. Then sewn by you. Every bowl had to be carved or turned and fired by...that's right, you, unless you knew someone who could do it for you. Everything you ate, you had to grow or trade for. The labor involved seems staggering. To think that this past Christmas, two clicks brought so much of my shopping to the door: sweaters, board games, fancy face creams, and, because I needed it last minute, even bleach. What used to take an entire day can now take a minute.

We headed back across the field and garden to the museum, as beautiful carillon music started up. Rich-ard told us how for almost 200 years, the carillon in the tower of the brick building yonder played the Angelus at noon.

"But that's not the Angelus," I said. "That's a Broad-way show tune!"

"I know," Richard said with a sigh. "This week it's from *Oklahoma*. The government owns the building now."

In the museum we studied detailed dioramas of how the Daughters of Charity nursed at Gettysburg, seven-teen miles away, along with their canteens, bandages, and bread-like field rations. One vignette showed a wounded soldier with a young nun kneeling over his dirty body, his face bloody. The diorama set them in dirt and grass, with a broken fence and bullets. The pretty nun looked a little too clean and starched, given her surroundings. Still, the point got across very well that these nuns walked through hell to help. I looked at Keely as she took in the scene, all twenty-one years of her, wondering if her year in the trenches of education would give her clarity on her own life's purpose. How I'd thought, at twenty-one, that lying on a beach in Greece would clarify for me my life's purpose. (Which it didn't. It did, however, narrow my options, forcing me to finally return to college.)

A young family stopped to also take in the diorama. The dad kneeled down and talked quietly to his little girl. "See, he had a bad owie, and she is making it better." His wife strolled up, wearing black leggings and a black stretchy dress, looking six months pregnant, and mused on the scene. She stroked her daughter's head.

"Daddy, why does he have an owie?" But Daddy had moved on to the next display. "Daddy, is his owie better? Daddy?" He turned around. "Yes, honey, she did make it better." The little girl with her tousled hair and pink dress took another thoughtful look and caught up with her mom and dad.

In displays, we saw Ann Seton's embroidered theater slippers and a formal miniature with her hair done up in ribbons, from when her life was good but before it became great. We then entered the huge and airy shrine. Quietly we made our way to her side altar, but darn—her body wasn't on display! I'd been mistaken. It's stashed behind a marble panel in the altar—not on view, never has been on view. However, a first-class relic of her was there. First-class means there's a piece of her body. But it is so, so small. Much smaller than a ladybug. The words around it, even with my #2 readers, were too tiny to be readable. Ah well.

Candles were available to light, a beautiful bank of them. All right. My intentions, like always, it seems, were that each of my daughters will develop into the full personhood God wants for them. That will eternally be my prayer. Actually, let me extend this prayer to all people everywhere: to have the opportunity to be the full person God wants for them. Yes. But, too, when I am in a sacred place, lots of different thoughts flood in and out of my mind. I loved a line in the movie *Rocket Man* about the life of Elton John. At his first performance in the United States, he got such intense stage fright that his manager yelled at him, "Become the person you were meant to be so that you can become the man you want to be! Now get out there!" How many of us have had stage fright in our own everyday lives, even when things are going, in fact, too well?

I stopped at the gift shop, a copy of *Saint Everywhere* with me, which I showed to Kathleen, the young woman not really in charge. "There's a chapter on Ann Seton," I said with pride. She looked it over carefully and said her manager would be interested. "Let me gift it to your manager," I said, and she said, "I think she'll love it."

With that, we said our goodbyes to St. Seton's shrine. Time to get back to DC and let adorable Keely prepare her lessons for the next day. She said there was always so much to do. And she told us that maybe she'd give teaching another year, as she had quite fallen in love with her students.

Generosity

A few years ago, I came across a *New York Times* review of a book called *On Kindness*, by Adam Phillips and Barbara Taylor. I thought, *Wow, that's great!* The gist of the review, by Peter Stevenson, was that we are psychologically afraid of our own and others' kindness. Stevenson wrote, quoting the authors, "We are battling back against our innate kindness, with which we are fairly bursting…. Why? Because 'real kindness is an exchange with essentially unpredictable consequences. It is a risk precisely because it mingles our needs and desires with the needs and desires of others.' By walling ourselves off from our inner kindness, we end up skulking around, hoarding scraps from the lost magical kindness of childhood, worried our hatred is stronger than our love." Stevenson later quotes the authors that this robs us of one of the great sources of human happiness.

These are strong words, and maybe you do not agree. But I decided to test it out.

I was having my picture professionally taken by a lovely woman. We got along great and were having fun. I'd brought a scarf, for a possible switch in look. I have loved scarves since I was a tiny child and have vivid memories of playing in my mother's scarf drawer. This one I'd bought in Italy. It had a scene of Florence painted on it. "What a beautiful scarf," she commented. "Let's take some shots wearing that."

"Thanks, it is beautiful, right?" She shot away with her complicated camera.

"The color is just so good," she commented again.

It sprang into my mind: *Do it. Give it to her. Just do it! You have so many scarves.* She finished shooting. Feeling consumed with spontaneity, I whisked the scarf off and held it out to her.

"It's yours. Please. I'd love for you to have it." Her expression changed, and she shook her head.

"It's beautiful, but no." I hadn't even considered that she wouldn't want it.

"Honestly, I mean it—if you only knew how many I have." We had just met each other. She sighed.

"No," she said graciously. "The thing is, I have had cancer, and I don't want a scarf if I don't need a scarf."

"Oh, I'm so sorry. I didn't know...." And feeling like a fool, I put my scarf back on. What an awkward situation! Suddenly I understood the book's premise perfectly. You do run a risk, but I consoled myself with the fact that it was an honest mistake, and better to try and die of humiliation than not try. And to be walled off from an urge toward generosity seemed bad to me.

New opportunities arise when you least expect them. Last summer, I popped into a boutique full of fun clothing. I happily browsed a rack of blouses. I happened to be wearing the last pair of earrings I still had that I'd made during my jewelry-making binge of 2002–2003, after my brother Jeff had died from complications of diabetes. Jeff was two years older than me. Everyone wanted to be around his brand of hilarity, his take on life. He was big and redheaded, and with one glance, we could break into uncontrollable laughter. They say it takes two years to recover from a close loss—not that the meaning of that person ever leaves you, but just to recover your equilibrium. For those two years, I feverishly made jewelry. Every woman for a hundred miles around seemed to get some of it. One regret from this time: Little Rosie was so young and wanted so much to help. She'd take all the best stones, turquoise and amber and amethyst, cram them all onto one "piece," and want to keep it for herself. I'd get cranky, say "No!" and make her undo it. To this day, as she makes her way into her grown-up life, how I wish I'd let her have them all. I acted out of scarcity when I could easily have acted out of abundance.

Anyway, I was wearing the last pair of earrings I still had from my time of mourning Jeff, and another shopper was browsing the same rack. We were both commenting on how great the stuff was when she admired my earrings. "Thanks, I made 'em," I said.

"Really?" she said, smiling but not looking at me. She was looking at the earrings. I was complimented. We began talking as we browsed. Women can easily chat while shopping side by side. She told me how her son was studying in Moscow for the summer—how hard it was for her, but she knew it was good for him. But really, couldn't it have been Miami? I felt for her. I'd been in that situation, too. And then...she admired my earrings again. My insides heated up. *Yes. No. No. Yes.* I wanted to...I wanted to be free and spontaneous. But I didn't know her at all! Then the words started just coming out of my mouth. First I said to her, "Just say yes." She was startled.

"Ah...yes?" she said, baffled. I whisked the earrings

out of my ears and held them out to her.

"No!" she said. "No. No." She put her hands behind her back. Crap—not this again.

"Yes, take them, please. I want you to have them." She was so uncomfortable. And now, so was I. She started backing away.

"I have so many—hundreds! I never really liked these." (Lie.) I stepped toward her just a little bit because she'd backed away. She was starting to look scared. Me, too. I wondered if she wouldn't take them out of embarrassment. Or maybe she actually hated them. How to get out of this? I pressed on, holding my hand out. What else was I going to do? Put them back in my ears and say "Sorry"? Finally, she realized the only way out was to accept them. And we both were so glad to be out of such an unexpectedly intense exchange. After brief smiles and a thank-you, we hurried away from each other.

Okay, that was another totally embarrassing failure of spontaneously giving something to someone who, it seemed, may like it. I believe it was humiliating for both of us. What's going wrong? Why is it so challenging to *freely* give and receive? Are we doomed to give in to these inner fears? I won't accept that, but on reflection, maybe those flubs stemmed from my not knowing either of these women. I couldn't tell the difference between pressing something upon someone and offering what would actually be appreciated. There's an art to giving gifts large and small. I hope to finesse future opportunities, whatever they may be, and to not shy away from them.

Seven

Saintly Hairdresser to High Society

VENERABLE PIERRE TOUSSAINT
1781–1853
Haiti and New York City

Bill is so funny. He enjoys a trip thoroughly, but only after he's comfortably *back home*. Thank goodness New York City is a place he loves. It holds so many family stories for us. Because of Bill's fascination with my family, he has done a great deal of research. We know my grandparents' very first address in America, from 1860, which is still there and only one block from the Tenement Museum. We know their last address, before departing, penniless, to California, which is still there and still so deluxe, up on Riverside Drive. They had to leave that place after the stock market crash of 1929. It's fun to check family facts like, *Was my grandmother Ruthie the Queen of the Coney Island Mardi Gras in 1912, or was it 1914? Was it the* New York Times *or* New York

Telegraph *that sponsored the contest?* (Thank you, New York Public Library.)

Recently, Bill and I went to New York because our oldest, Glennie, now thirty-one, was on a work assignment. She's with Weight Watchers, or WW as it's now called. And I was excited for the chance to get to know Pierre Toussaint, dubbed the Holy Hairdresser. He was, in fact, the most sought-after coiffeur of his day. His clients were at the pinnacle of society. He is a somehow saint—his cause for canonization opened in 1953, one hundred years after his death.

New York in November: cold, rainy, and getting dressed up for Christmas. "Sure, I'll spend the day with you and Dad, poking around Manhattan looking for your somehow saint," Glennie said. So with Bill commanding Google Maps, we headed on foot toward lower Manhattan and Mulberry Street to find Toussaint's first grave. Oh, the wonderful chaos of New York's streets, the jackhammers, pastry shops, dry cleaners, crowds hurrying, and...the aroma of roasting chestnuts!

"Mom, tell me who he was," Glennie asked as we hurried along, shoulder to shoulder. All six-foot-five of Bill, ahead, would stop, look up and down, turn the phone this way and that, and then keep going as we simply followed.

"Let's see. Well, Glennie, he was born a slave in Haiti. To be a slave anywhere is terrible, but in Haiti it was worse." I rolled off the unhappy litany: the constant heat, the hurricanes, the earthquakes, the yellow fever, the typhus. Haiti imported more slaves each year than any other European colony, and the death rate was so high that fresh labor had to be constantly coming in.

Glennie wrinkled her brow. This is not the benign saint story she was expecting. "Harvesting sugar is really physically hard, and the sugar-curing jars were where the mosquitoes that carried the yellow fever bred," I continued.

"That's unbelievable," Glennie said.

I replied, "I know." We hurried to keep up with Bill.

Pierre was born into being a house slave, so he was better off than most. His family had lived on the Bérard plantation for generations, and, in fact, his grandmother was so trusted by the Bérards that she was the one who chaperoned the family's children back and forth to France, where they attended school. After the family granted her her freedom, she stayed on as the plantation's majordomo. So Pierre had an advantaged place, comparatively speaking. As a small child, he was so winning that everyone considered him the little love of the plantation. He could mimic anyone, make anyone laugh. Marie Bérard, wife of the plantation owner, Jean-Jacques, made sure Pierre was taught to read and write. Being French, the Bérards were Catholic, and so, too, were their slaves. Pierre really learned about Catholicism, though, by reading the sermons of French Jesuits in the plantation library as he dusted all the other books. By the time Pierre was nine, he was a valet, learning the ins and outs of clothing, fashions, fabrics, what looked good with what.

"How could they have loved him if they still made him be their slave?" Glennie asked.

Shaking my head, I went on, "I don't know. I'm sure

it wouldn't pass for that now, but a lot is known about the emotions of the family, from letters written across all their lifetimes. Letters from Pierre, the Bérards, the aunts and uncles who fled to France or to Cuba, and from other slaves, freed, who ended up in Baltimore."

When Pierre was a teenager, I told her, the Bérards fled to New York. The Haitian slave revolt that became the Haitian Revolution was well under way. Jean-Jacques had tried to remain neutral, but as the bloodshed escalated to mass slaughter on both sides, they finally got out, bringing Pierre, his little sister, Rosalie, and three other house slaves with them.

When they arrived in 1797, New York City was full of hustle and optimism. From the dock, if the family had taken transport up Wall Street, which was the main thoroughfare, they would have passed the large home at 57 Wall Street. Pierre could never have guessed that in a few years he would be an anticipated friend and an essential attendant to the wife and granddaughters there. It was the home of Alexander Hamilton.

New York was filling up with aristocrats fleeing the French Revolution and, now, the French colonialists or "Creoles" fleeing Haiti. Today, "Creole" means of mixed white and black descent, especially from the Caribbean, but originally it meant, simply, French colonists. New Yorkers thought this influx was great because, in that day and place, the manners and language of high culture were French. Pierre spoke perfect French—this was an entree to the upper crust.

Once the Bérards had settled, Jean-Jacques told Pierre, age sixteen, that he needed to have a trade in their new life in America. He arranged for Pierre to apprentice with a popular ladies' hairdresser. Jean-Jacques said he could keep the money he earned.

"That was *nice* of his master," Glennie said with plenty of sarcasm as we kept pace with Bill.

Mrs. King requests Mr. Toussaint to call on her at No. 56 Bond St. at 6 o'clock tomorrow afternoon to dress her for Miss Ming's ball.

We women with our hair.... Since forever, women have sought what's new in hairstyles. First it was powdered and piled high. Then low with coils and curls. Pierre figured it out and learned quickly. He understood style and trends, and in those days, wealthy women could spend upward of $1,000 a year on hairdressing. Many had their coiffeurs on retainer, with daily visits. Soon, society's leading ladies wanted only Pierre. We know this from letters written between these women. They loved him! His impeccable manners, his dress, his perfect French. He had this jovial, witty charm. But the letters go on to say how much his clients anticipated his appointments because he was somebody they could really talk to. He didn't gossip and was so discreet that these women felt him to be a true confidant. When pressed for gossip (as no doubt he heard plenty!) he would tactfully say that he was "no news journal." And Pierre offered encouragement and words of wisdom to these women about their privileged stations in life, helping them realize opportunities to be of service to others. They wrote about feeling inspired and uplifted by him. In time Pierre formed true friendships across social boundaries, one of which led to the biography of him written shortly after his death.

"You know, Glennie, your great-grandmother *loved* her hairdressers, too! She went every Friday at three o'clock," I said. I described the platinum-blond bubble that Ruthie wore decade after decade. She'd wrap it in toilet paper every night so it stayed hard and shiny. We kids would laugh so hard when she came around in the morning with bits of TP still hanging there. Ruthie lived with us, in the garage my dad converted to comfortable quarters. She'd have coffee in the kitchen and study the newspaper while we ate our cereal, a part of her job selling newspaper ads.

Pierre attended daily Mass at St. Peter's, the only Catholic church in the city. People remarked about his deep faith. He spoke with ease about this faith to mistrustful Protestants. It was very natural to him because, after all, in Haiti everyone was Catholic.

As the years progressed, Pierre became more and more affluent. He kept his ears open. He invested in property. He invested in insurance companies. He was excellent at saving. Early on, he also began giving to those in need. When he wasn't hurrying from one client to the next, Pierre was in the streets, helping those at the opposite end of society. In those days, the streets teemed with people in dire distress: street children, freed slaves, those struggling for freedom, confused newcomers, the sick, and the lame. He offered money, assistance, friendship, and words of encouragement to countless people he sought out or encountered. By now, I could tell I had Glennie's full attention. "What so many of his friends commented upon in the letters was how kind he was and the 'quality of his heart.' "

Bill turned around to face us, exasperated. "I think just two more blocks," he said. "This darn thing is so confused on the walk function. If you put it in your pocket, or put your hand down, it forgets where it is." We wrapped our scarves around our necks, the wind blew leaves across the street, and I hoped it wouldn't rain. We were passing fun little shops along Mulberry Street, and I wanted coffee in someplace warm, but we were on a mission. I wanted to learn more, too, about why a slave who finally got something to call his own— *money*—would be so generous with it.

Jean-Jacques died when he returned to Haiti to attempt to rescue their plantation wealth. This left his cheerful, socialite wife, Marie, penniless in New York. Pierre began quietly supporting her, paying her bills. He was doing so well as a hairdresser that he also bought his sister's freedom. Rosalie would be free to marry, and her children would be born free—Pierre wanted this very much for her. He also gave her a dowry.

"That's amazing! Then what?" asked Glennie. I'd gotten stopped by a store window full of fabric from Nepal. New York is heaven for the ADD mind. "Mom, Mom—go on!" she insisted.

"Listen to this: He buys his sister's freedom, then he buys the freedom of another Haitian slave, Juliette Noel, whom he later married. But meanwhile poor Madame Marie, his owner, had become so depressed. It was Pierre who brought her sweets and treats and encouraged her to give parties to cheer herself up.

Though we don't understand it, there was great affection and loyalty between the two of them. When Marie
gave Pierre her jewels to sell to pay the bills, he came
back with the money and the jewels, saying he had
taken care of it. *Can you believe it?* Marie eventually
remarried a Mr. Nicolas. But Mr. Nicolas didn't have
money either, so now Pierre was supporting Marie and
her second husband."

Glennie scoffed. "Why would he do that!"

"And it gets more amazing," I said, feeling like
Scheherazade, with an inexhaustible supply of stories.
"When she was dying, Marie granted Pierre his freedom. She and Mr. Nicolas took him to the French con-
sulate and signed all the papers emancipating him. As
he had been born in Haiti, this now made Pierre a full
French citizen. When Marie finally did die—Pierre
then supported Mr. Nicolas."

Glennie stopped and stamped her foot. "He's got no
responsibility to that second husband!"

We had arrived at Old St. Patrick's on Mulberry
Street. This is not the monumental "new" St. Patrick's,
on 5th Avenue, the one that attracts five million visitors a year. No, this quiet, old, red-stone church, surrounded by an ancient graveyard, speaks to an almost
vanished New York. Yellow, orange, and brown leaves
fell on the headstones like confetti. The graveyard was
locked. We entered Old St. Patrick's, of glorious wood
and paint, through the side door and looked for someone to ask for help. Bill finally spotted a man with a big
ring of keys on his belt, changing out all the burned-
down votive candles on a side altar. John, his name

was, and he walked us back out to the cemetery gate.

"I am so sorry, closed today," he said in a Polish accent.

"We came to see Pierre Toussaint's marker," I asked, pleadingly. It was about to rain. Our shoes were damp. John nodded, wanting to be helpful, but locked meant locked. He pointed through the wrought-iron fence, saying, "Look past this big white headstone right here. See the cement obelisk beyond it?" We nodded. "Now look to the ground. See the triangle sticking up?" The three of us gasped. Yes, yes, there it was in the grass! Like a giant loaf of bread. Proof that this unbelievably kind, heroic man wasn't a myth. But no one, unless they were informed, would notice that marker.

"He was buried here until 1996," John said. "He was one of the most generous donors for the construction of this church, but he didn't attend here. They would not bury a black man where he did attend, at St. Peter's, so he was laid to rest here at St. Patrick's." We thanked John for sharing his time with us and stood at the fence, looking through for a while. I wished Gracie and Rosie could be with us on this funny version of a family outing, but they were in California, at work. Not so long ago my children and I were always together in the car, running errands or going somewhere fun, all of them tucked into car seats or boosters. The great Judy McCord, a mentor in my community on motherhood and spirituality, said something once that never left me. She said it in jest, but not really: "Raising children is like pushing a boulder uphill. You get to the top, and then it rolls away."

At twenty-nine, when his mistress died, Pierre became a free man. Now able to marry, he bought a house at 144 Franklin Street for himself and Juliette, who was fifteen. Together they had a cheerful and loving home. When his beloved sister Rosalie died of tuberculosis, they adopted her daughter, little Euphemie, and gave her the best of everything. There is a lovely, ivory miniature of Euphemie at age thirteen in the New York Historical Society. She would die of tuberculosis, too, at age fourteen. Her death seemed only to redouble Pierre's and Juliette's acts of generosity.

"Let's go see the church he attended Mass in," I said. "Bill, can you find our way to St. Peter's on Barclay?" Onward, another two miles to the Lower West Side. Walking, we feasted our eyes on the shop signs: NO BULL CLEAN FOODS. DIRTY HANDS JEWELRY—*HAND-MADE*. And the awnings. Red awnings. Torn awnings. Striped awnings. But now, it was actually raining. My poncho performed so poorly that we stopped at a Mr. Banta's umbrella kiosk—also, Mr. Banta's perfumes, Mr. Banta's ties, Mr. Banta's hairbands. Mr. Banta was from Pakistan, and he was smiling. "I'll take a clear umbrella, so I can see through it," I said. Ten dollars and I was set. He waved goodbye so cheerfully that I realized how rain must make umbrella salesmen smile.

Halfway to St. Peter's, Bill discovered that we could find 144 Franklin Street. It wouldn't be far, so we changed course. From this address, Pierre and Juliette ran a small lending bank, an employment office, a way station for traveling priests, and a refuge for struggling newcomers. From here, Pierre raised the funds for Ann

Seton's first orphanage for boys, for the first order of black sisters, the Oblates, and for the new St. Vincent de Paul center. Pierre and Juliette offered assistance to former slaves. They took in destitute black boys and raised them like their own, schooling them in trades so they could fend for themselves. Pierre used his contacts to place the boys in good jobs.

Many of the white people they helped were society people or French émigrés who found themselves embarrassingly poverty stricken. Pierre knew how quickly society turned on someone in trouble. He devised ingenious plans for them: taking their unnecessary items and raffling them to others or holding small auctions for an unnamed party. He saw the isolation the wealthy were often trapped in, as he had unique access to the private areas of their homes and dressing rooms.

His friend Sarah Ann Moore wrote:

> *Dear Toussaint,*
> *I have been very sick, but am getting well enough to begin to think of making myself handsome again. Will you come this afternoon at 6 p.m. to cut and curl my hair so that I may be fit to show myself in the parlour tomorrow.*

As his faith instructed, he desired to be of help to all, and his heart did not narrow by sect or color, nor by poverty or wealth.

In 1803, while still a slave himself, Pierre famously crossed the quarantine line during the yellow fever epidemic, when 5,000 had already died and most doctors in New York couldn't take it anymore and had fled the city. He went down the lonely streets to find those still left in their houses and nursed them. Having come from Haiti, he'd had experience with yellow fever. It wasn't always fatal, but it was gruesome—another name for it was "the black vomit."

He crossed barriers, barricades, and boundaries easily, always to help. He wasn't stuck in the sort of mindset that I recently overheard from two women walking by: "If they like me, I like them. If they don't like me, I don't like them." What a poverty of philosophy compared with Pierre's.

Bill, Glennie, and I soon found ourselves standing in front of 144 Franklin. "This is kind of disappointing," Glennie said. Sadly, the Touissant townhouse is gone, along with the others like it. A brick-faced commercial building constructed around the turn of the last century stands there now. But my imagination conjured some details. How bustling Franklin and Broadway would have been in Pierre's time: clanging horse-drawn trams, pushcarts, two-seater buggies getting cut off by draft horses pulling wagon loads in what had just become the biggest city in the country. We stood for a moment before the brass numbers, 144, knowing Pierre would have come in and out multiple times a day over the forty-plus years he lived there. Every single day he walked to 6 a.m. Mass at St. Peter's, a mile away. And that was our next stop.

But first, it was seriously time to get out of the wet and the wind. And ahh, before long we were in a warm, cozy spot with steaming chai tea, a cappuccino, and a hot chocolate before us. Bill and I stared at

Glennie, the way parents do, never getting enough of her, especially now that she lives far away. Bill smiled broadly. He was relaxing. "Okay, Pierre was amazing," Bill commented with actual admiration, surprising me because while he is obliging, saints are not really his thing. "I am having a great time," he added. Glennie and I gave each other a wink. Rare words from him.

The rain let up. It was time to carry on to St. Peter's. Upon arriving, we took the steep granite steps up to the main entrance. When the original burned down in the Great Fire of 1835, Pierre became a financial leader in rebuilding this massive Greek Revival-style replacement. The large cemetery that once surrounded St. Peter's is now a Four Seasons hotel and several high-rises. Maybe Pierre would be glad he wasn't buried here after all, because today those graves are long gone. Pierre stayed well marked and safe at Old St. Patrick's from 1853 until 1996.

Standing at the entrance of St. Peter's, we were surprised by a bronze plaque right at the front door, next to Ann Seton's, explaining how Pierre Toussaint had been a devout, generous, and pious parishioner for sixty-six years. Looking across to the street sign, high on its post, I saw that, yes, it is Barclay Street—but sharing the green street sign are the words: "Pierre Toussaint Square." I hadn't noticed that from my first visit, but today I was looking for it. It's like the city of New York was sending out a postcard from the long-ago past, spelling it out for us today: *We as a city remember him. We know what he did. He made a difference.* It's funny to think that a person's good deeds can shine so long after they are gone—for Pierre, 170 years already. They offer a light to me, to us, on the way to be.

Pierre had prejudice to contend with from every direction. Most African Americans were Protestant, and at that time, Protestants white and black were prejudiced against Catholics. White Catholics, meanwhile, were prejudiced against blacks. Thus he was part of a minuscule minority within a minority. But his magnetic personality, his intelligence, and obvious goodness allowed many to see him for the person he really was.

So many struggle to be seen for who they are. My mom was never freed from being the good daughter of an alcoholic. Thank goodness she could sneak away at night to be loud or silly or dramatic in community theater. My sister Sally was finally freed from being a buttoned-down banker to flourish as a scrappy estate dealer. My brother Kevin is gay, always was gay, but not free to be himself until almost middle age.

Pierre said he had only one master, and that was God. From the time of his youth, he never thought of himself as anything less than a child of God and therefore divinely protected. In reading about him, I came again to the word *holy*, which comes from *whole*, as in free from wound or injury.

Pierre was known for his ease in speaking about his faith. He could quote the Sermon on the Mount, the Beatitudes, and much else by heart. Jesus taught that we must live to a higher standard than mere law or society requires. The law says you shall not kill, but Jesus instructed his followers to go deeper—if you are even *angry* at your fellow, for no cause, you have done wrong. Pierre spoke of how Jesus replaced "an eye for an eye" with "turn the other cheek," spoke of how a man cannot serve two masters. Small groups often gathered to listen closely.

As he came closer, in his long life, to the time of the Civil War, Pierre was asked many times to get involved in the fight for emancipation. He said emancipation was a blessing, and he paid for the freedom of many people. But he had seen so much torture and bloodshed in Haiti, he didn't want to see more.

Obvious goodness: We know it when we see it, in all its endless ways. Pierre understood that our work here on earth is to help relieve suffering and raise up those around us. He just quietly gave and gave of himself. He knew how to make money, and he knew what to do with it. All of us right now could make a call to help someone get a better job, or have someone to our table for a good and cheery meal, or give away a little money. Pierre did this day in and day out. There's a funny account of how Pierre helped a proud man, whom he secretly knew to be almost destitute. He had Juliette cook fine French food and wrap it as if from a restaurant. He would secretly deliver it to him. Then when he saw the man, Pierre would ask him how he was getting on. The man would say, "Oh, fine! Very well indeed. Can you not see how well I am eating? I have so many friends." The account goes on to say what delight Juliette and Pierre took in their secret acts.

There was one more stop on our long amble through Pierre Toussaint's Manhattan. We caught the subway and headed north, emerging twenty-five minutes later

at 53rd and 5th, across the street from St. Patrick's Cathedral, the very heart of Manhattan's billion-dollar
real estate. Rockefeller Center's ice rink was across the
street. Saks 5th Avenue, next door.

How often, since my twenties, has the phrase:
"Let's rendezvous on the steps of St. Patrick's," been
said between me and friends, me and family. It's way
easier to meet there than, say, at the Eiffel Tower—my
screwball idea in 1973, when I tried to meet my brother
Kevin at an equally iconic spot. St. Patrick's you can't
miss. A flight of granite steps up to 9,000-pound bronze
doors. In Paris, honestly, it took two days, because we
didn't know the Eiffel Tower had four legs—well, we
knew that, but we didn't understand that each leg
was almost a city block apart. Try meeting up *there* in
the pre-cell-phone era. I'd been in Europe six months
already, but poor Kevin had just landed. He'd never
been anywhere in his whole life except the beach. He
was so anxious, looking for me, that he'd pulled out
a significant part of his beard. Being a loving sister, I
right away laughed and blurted out, "What the heck
happened to your beard?" Had we not connected within one more hour, he would've found a way back to
the airport and flown straight home. Except he had
already been pickpocketed.

My heart soared, entering St. Patrick's Cathedral.
I nudged Bill and Glennie to come with me to light
candles. "Glennie, have I told you—"

"Yes, Mom. Like every time we come here. Your
mother had her First Communion here in 1926." I
smiled to myself; of course I had told her.

This is Pierre's final resting place. Because of popular devotion, Cardinal O'Connor had Pierre exhumed from Old St. Patrick's in 1996. He paid him the highest of honors, as a layman, and had him interred here, where only cardinals and archbishops are buried. Later, he had Juliette buried at Pierre's side. We passed all the side altars for saints and stepped reverently back behind the main, high altar. There, across from the Lady Chapel, are the steps to the crypt. A prayer in a brass holder is bolted to the marble railing, a prayer for the canonization of Pierre Toussaint. Leaning, you can see past a locked gate to Pierre's brass plaque in the wall, at the bottom of the steps. I knelt down and said the prayer, realizing again how canonizations begin with prayer. Then I continued with my own addition:

> *Pierre Toussaint, help me be more holy. Let us follow*
> *your example of bringing love to whoever is in need*
> *with no notice of color or religion. Bless our country.*
> *By your example bring us together.*

As he grew to old age, people would say, "Pierre, why don't you relax and enjoy your money? You have plenty!"

"I do have plenty for myself, but if I stopped working, I wouldn't have enough for everyone else!" he'd reply with a smile.

When Pierre died in 1853, what happened is what so often happens at funerals. Those who attended were astonished at the crowd—from the richest to the poorest, from the most important to the invisible.

Obituary excerpts from newspapers in July 1853:

Pierre Toussaint for more than sixty years had been the most respected and beloved Negro in New York…a testimony to the beauty and force of character. Known for his long watchfulness and kind attentions at the bedside of the sick and the departing. Thus goodness springing from refined and elevated principle…devoting himself to social and benevolent duty….

Venerable Pierre Toussaint. "Venerable" means a person who lived a heroically virtuous life and pursued holiness while here on earth. What a good thing to pursue, holiness, as in whole and without injury. Whole to be everything you really are.

And a final quote from the future saint:

I have never felt I am a slave to any man or woman, but I am a servant of Almighty God who made us all. When one of His children is in need, I am glad to be His slave.

Salina

I never tell anyone where I get my hair done. My friends and daughters spend so much money getting their hair to look just great, but I've taken to running over to Supercuts. Especially now that I've had to show up presentable for so many book events. When I discovered that you can call for an appointment, go with your hair wet, and get a speedy blow dry—in and out—in thirty minutes, it became my weekly thing. Hair can be such a pain.

One time, Lucero, the stylist who'd been doing such a great job, wasn't there. I was assigned to someone named Salina. Drat! Who's this Salina person?

In no time, I was under a black cape in her twirly chair. Salina looked like she'd seen a lot of life already. Her eyeliner blue, her lips a kind of magenta, her full, long, black hair neon green at the ends. Tattoos everywhere, even a soft, heart-shape one under her chin. Every time she raised her arm while blow-drying the top of my head, a big, suffering face of Jesus with large drops of blood revealed itself. There was so much suffering on that face of Jesus on Salina's underarm. "Oh my gosh," I said. "That tattoo's amazing. Let me see better." She held her arm aloft proudly.

"It's really art, right?" she said. With that amount of emotion captured by the tattooist, I could not disagree. Even though, ugh, all that blue ink....

"Why, Salina—why Christ on your arm?"

"It's my happy arm! See, it's my mother below

Christ. And all the things I love: roses, hearts..."

"What's written above Jesus's head?"

"'Who do you say I am?' You know, that part in the Bible," she explained, "when Peter asks, 'Are you a prophet? Are you the messiah? Who are you?'"

"Oh," I said, a bit embarrassed. In fact, I didn't know. Salina then showed me a shoulder with *Matt 5:12* tattooed on it.

"I have a lot of opportunity to speak the word because of my tattoos," she said. "I didn't know that's what would happen when I started getting them, but people are curious, you know. Like you," she said, blow-drying away without missing a beat.

"And what's that one, up your other arm?" All I could see was part of a bird pecking at—seeds?

"Oh, the parable of the sower."

"The mustard seeds," I offered happily.

"Well, no. The sower," she said patiently. She took her arm out of her sweater. The parable played out all the way up her arm: seeds being eaten by birds, seeds sprouting and wilting, seeds blooming with bad thorns, and finally, across her shoulder, roses blooming abundantly (in fertile soil). "Once I almost got vampires up my arm, and at the last minute I thought—wait!—what would I say about them for the rest of my life?" I gave her a mom's-nod of approval for good decision-making.

"Show me whatever you can show me," I asked, thoroughly enjoying our interaction. She pulled the neck of her sweater away. On her collarbone was *Philippians 1:21*. I nodded like I knew what that referred to. "Salina," I asked, "what's cool for you about doing hair?"

She thought a minute. "It's art," she said. "All the things you can do with color! I love making such a difference in someone's appearance. Usually people feel so good when they leave."

I nodded again, this time knowing exactly what she was talking about. Why is it we feel so beautiful, so invincible, when we leave a hair salon?

Back in my car, I Googled *Philippians 1:21*: "For me to live is Christ. To die is gain." Google said these are among the most memorable words in the Bible. I have trouble understanding them. I'd go home and look into it more. Then I Googled the first part of *Matthew 5:12*: "Rejoice and be glad, for great is your reward." Okay, that part's easy to grasp. Salina gained by being able to speak the word to me. I had gained, too. But she is the one who made the effort, who put herself in the position of possible ridicule, not me.

I drove out of the parking lot thinking about her tattoos. It's like she'd stamped a personal "Never Lost" system onto herself, permanent GPS settings toward her own personal highway to heaven. Amazing.

Eight

Drying Her Cloak on a Sunbeam

St. Brigid of Kildare

451–524
Ireland

Our trip began even before we'd left the kitchen. While Bill was making eggs, a call came in from Ireland. The lovely, lilting voice of a woman named Rachel was at the other end warning us, along with all the people who'd booked rooms at the Cunningham, that electricity would be off for the day after we arrived. No light, no heat.

Bill was instantly alarmed. When I hung up, he said, "We've got to rebook someplace else right now." For some reason I just told him, *No, let's not rush, it will be okay.* Bill quickly looked up the temperature in Kildare for two days hence—thirty-eight degrees. "Mary Lea, how is this going to be okay?" I gave a little shrug, not knowing either.

We were headed to Italy to meet up with friends,

to experience Carnevale in Venice. What good fortune to have found an excellent price on round-trip tickets that gave us a four-day layover in Ireland at no extra charge! Here was a chance to discover another saint, and who else but St. Brigid of Kildare? It had bothered me that in New York City, St. Patrick gets the mega-church and St. Brigid gets the little parish church, yet she is also a patron saint of Ireland, right along with him. And her name was so common among immigrants to America that it became synonymous with a young Irish housemaid—as in, "Don't worry, I'll have my Brigid bring it to you." Brigid is venerated for the protection of hearth and home. In Ireland, her distinctive straw cross in the form of a zigzag adorns shop windows and doorways and is stuccoed onto buildings. Every tchotchke shop is laden with her blessings decoupaged onto plaques and tea towels. Brigid is wondrously intertwined with the misty beginnings of Ireland itself, and her influence is still very much alive.

Because before there was St. Brigid, there was simply Brigid (or Bríg or Bhrid), the Celtic triple goddess of higher ground, higher learning, and higher consciousness. Revered by the ancient Celts in all of Britain, she was the goddess of fire, of fertility, of abundance, of poetry. Centuries before the emergence of Christianity and our St. Brigid, the priestesses of Brigid tended her pagan flame temple in the woods on the hill above what is today Kildare—Cill Dara, Church of the Oak. Brigid's church among the oaks.

Kildare is forty-five minutes east of the Dublin airport on the M5 motorway, but I'm sure Bill aged way more than that getting us there. The night we landed, oh, the wind and the rain came down! And then the darn driving on the wrong side of the road. I navigated, but I don't see that well at night anymore. He had both hands on the steering wheel. I had both hands clutching the phone. Neither of us said anything but *Get ready to merge. What's next? The right lane now. How far? One-point-five kilometers. Get over. Coming up quick*, etc. The rain blinded the windshield. *Lord! We are too old for this.*

When we finally got to our lodgings, the first order of business was a half pint of Guinness and a seat by the fire of the pub next door. This pub was heaven—the happy noise, the way everyone knew one another, big bear-hug greetings, the young and old traipsing back and forth to hang with this friend here, then that friend there. The little fire dancing merrily at our feet. Wow, so happy just to be there.

Kildare is the second, or third, oldest city in Ireland, more than 1,500 years old, and was founded by St. Brigid herself. She arrived in 480 with her group of nuns and decided to build on an oak-covered hill overlooking the Curragh (*COOR-ah*) plains. Here she founded the most important of her monasteries—her double monastery, for both men and women—and as years passed, the scriptorium, then the art and metal school. Over time, it became known as the great monastery of Kildare, and the town forming around it grew to be a market town, then a cathedral town, and, in recent history, adding woolen mills, military, and—its huge claim to fame—the sport of kings, horse racing.

The Irish Derby is held at the historic Curragh race-track on lands that once were part of St. Brigid's fields. Horse breeding came to Kildare with the Knights Hospitaller in 1150. Also known as the Black Knights, they built their Black Abbey here, and the perfecting of thoroughbreds has been going on ever since. Today the Irish National Stud and Gardens are on the abbey's grounds, where ruins still stand. We learned all this from a convivial bunch of guys next to us in the pub who were jockeys and handlers.

I excitedly told them how I'd come to learn what I could about St. Brigid. This did not impress them. It made them laugh. "Do ya not have Google in California, then?" one of them said. Bill and I laughed, too. Were we like the tourists who come to Hollywood hoping to see traces of Marilyn Monroe?

The jewel of the town of Kildare is the Cathedral of St. Brigid, the former site of her monastery and cathedral—but with the great suppression of the Catholic church in the sixteenth century under Henry VIII, it fell into total ruin until the 1890s, when it reemerged as Anglican. That was our goal for the next morning. We put on our warmest clothes before stepping out into the wind, a wind that turned out to be our friend—because of it, the local electric utility had delayed its planned outages in case they had to deal with unplanned ones. Two short blocks of little Irish shops took us right up to the cathedral's iron gates.

This hill is among the most important religious sites in Ireland. Where the cathedral stands was the goddess Brigid's sanctuary. The words *druid* and *pagan* are a little scary to me, sounding rather like words to stay away from. But in the context of ancient Celtic spirituality, which imbued nature with spiritual properties worthy of veneration, these words lose their ominousness. And too, St. Brigid was the daughter of a pagan chieftan, though her mother was a slave and a Christian. This all echoed St. Kateri for me, though centuries and cultural worlds apart.

One theory of how Brigid's mother was a Christian is that she had been abducted from Portugal by Irish raiders. Brigid, however, was schooled by her father's people. It's possible she was even one of the priestesses who tended the goddess Brigid's eternal flame on the hill. But when she met Patrick, she was open to and understanding of Christian principles. She was able to convert the women around her, as she understood both sides of this Celtic coin.

Brigid's religious beginnings happened so early in history that nothing was written down. Symbols and hash marks, like the runes of other northern European peoples, were the only written language. Some of this early symbol-language, mostly found carved into stone, has been translated into wonderfully startling poetry.

And the lark said in her song
Often, often, often,
Goes the Christ in a stranger's guise.

So this cathedral site is where St. Brigid founded her double monastery and where she was head abbess. She invited men to lead the monks, but she was in charge. Her schools attracted young women and men from all over Ireland, and as the centuries passed, the scholars and theologians from Kildare spread out across northern Europe to evangelize and rekindle Christianity, which had all but disappeared in the early Dark Ages. Upon her death, Brigid was succeeded by other women. The monastery at Kildare would be headed by women for the next 600 years. This female leadership, and the idea of paired men's and women's monasteries, was unique at that time in Europe. The Celts, interestingly, had always had women in roles beyond that of wife and mother. Some were warriors, like Queen Maeve. But still, St. Brigid was unique in her position of authority.

We entered the cathedral grounds, with its spreading graveyard full of tall headstones and Celtic crosses. Brigid's original building materials were wood, sticks, and wattle, which would be destroyed and rebuilt constantly. Then fine stone construction began in the twelfth century. The cathedral was rebuilt again in the sixteenth century, then totally rebuilt again in the late nineteenth century. It has a square tower and four pitched wings coming out in each direction, solid and fortress-like, as if it were its own landform.

Yesterday we were in twenty-first-century Pasadena, California; today, in sixteenth-century Kildare. I breathed in the cold, sharp air. Barren hazelnut trees, their branches like varicose veins reaching across the sky, bent in the wind. The wet grass rippled. I'd heard about the idea of Ireland's "thin" places—places where you can feel something special, something spiritual, otherworldly even, where the veil between this world and another is very...thin. We kept our heads down against the cold and hurried across the graveyard to the cathedral's entrance. We took our seats for the 11:30 Anglican Mass. That morning, Rev. Tim would preach from the gospel of Matthew, the verses about salt and light.

Only a little bit of the cathedral is original from the twelfth century, but the restoration is perfect—gray, stacked heavy stone, arched oak ceiling, tall, thin windows—thus we were sitting amid stonework echoing back to Norman times. Over the centuries, St. Brigid's monastery was battered by no fewer than fifteen Viking attacks and countless sackings by local Irish kings. Monasteries were special targets because of their wealth. Display cases in back, where we entered, held things found in the ground nearby: a Neolithic stone ax head from around 4,000 BC, shards of pottery, remains of wax seals.

It was amazing to sit and listen to Rev. Tim preach, here, right here, where Christians have found inspiration since the earliest times. St. Matthew's gospel says we are to be the salt of the earth—you do not need much salt to make food taste better, and it is salt that helps keep food from going bad. So we are to be the salt.... And part two, we are to let our light shine. I've always loved this teaching—do not hide your light under a bushel basket—because in my life, I have so often hidden. It's that unhelpful mindset that if I were to "win" at something, then someone else would "lose." Well, how can a person get anywhere thinking like that? No. This gospel instructs us to use our gifts! Matthew's been exhorting us to do this for 2,000 years.

Hearing that gospel in this particular spot, with the heavy stone walls and oak roof, the wind howling in the trees outside, drew me into ancient, ancient times. I could almost see knights in chainmail at the doors. Crossbows in the slit windows of the round tower outside. It wasn't hard to envision myself in that world, sitting in this pew. I slid into contemplating how my writing life had cracked open relatively late in life. How I realized that if I didn't take my writing and desire for self-expression out of hiding, I'd be taking it to the grave with me—never having given one of my heart's desires (another name for gifts) its due. I highly recommend that if some unrealized desire hides in the shadow of your heart, you should stand up to your hesitation, embrace whatever it is, and dally no more.

Toward the back of the graveyard stands a 300-foot-high round tower from the fifth century, as well as the foundation of St. Brigid's flame temple. Flame temple? Yes. What one sees amid the medieval tombs and headstones is a rock foundation that from Neolithic times was the spot where Bríd and her priestesses—and then, in unbroken succession, St. Brigid and her sisters—tended the eternal flame that symbolically brings light to the great dark. The sisters tended their flame for 800 years, for sure, and possibly all the way until the sixteenth century. The temple foundation—you can step down into it—is rectangular and about the size of a large hotel Jacuzzi. I couldn't resist stepping into it, this immortal fire pit, my mind abuzz with its significance.

The next day, Bill took the car and drove off to

the city of Birr to see old friends, Skip and Kathleen, who'd moved to Ireland twenty years earlier. Patricia, a kind older lady in the tourist office in Kildare's town square, directed me on foot out to Solas Bhride—Brigid's Flame—a spirituality center run by the Brigidine sisters. The order, suppressed in the sixteenth century, was revived in 1807. Before suppression, they'd been going strong for over a thousand years. I wanted a taxi, but Patricia said, "No dear, walk. It's only twenty minutes." I looked doubtfully out at the wind, the light snow flurries. "It's a lovely walk—maybe it's only fifteen minutes." She smiled encouragingly.

I wiggled my toes to remind myself which shoes I was wearing. "Okay," I said, not wanting her to know that I felt a little afraid to walk out into the country on the side of the road by myself. She told me to make a left, go a little way, make a right, and then straight on.

Well, after twenty minutes, with snow flurries now turned to rain, I could see the spirituality center, but far, far on the other side of the paddocks of the National Stud farm. I was out there completely alone. My umbrella was blowing inside out. I'd taken the wrong right. I put my head down and marched on, just pretending I was in the fifth century. My puffy coat was becoming sodden. I wished it were a big ol' billowy woolen cape. *Rain never hurt anyone*, I told myself. *Think what women did in Brigid's time. And, umm, how pretty the green is in the rain. Maybe this is the way to St. Brigid's well, too.* There were at least fifteen sacred wells attributed to St. Brigid throughout the country. Healing wells. She used them to baptize people. People used them to cure their physical and spiritual woes and as nature spots at which to pray.

Maybe Bill and I would go look for the one near here—*by car*—tomorrow. Was my coat getting ruined? Why didn't I have a woolen cape? I'd seen one in a shop window. I wanted one. But I live in California. Could I wear it for Halloween? These thoughts carried me on until I finally arrived, just as the rain and the wind stopped.

The Solas Bhride is a serene, modern retreat center dedicated to the spirit of the saint. The sisters had planted daffodils in pots by the entrance in honor of Brigid's feast day, February 1, which had just passed—and of Imbolc (*EM-bug*), the pagan fest of the beginning of spring. They are unabashed by Brigid's pagan beginnings and, in fact, embody a poetic enfolding of the two. They welcome groups and solo travelers from all over the world, offering a hermitage, cottages, workshops, and conferences.

I was greeted at the door by Sister Phil. "Ah, come in, dearie, are you the one from the tourist office?" I nodded and stripped off my soggy coat. "Lovely day today. Come in and warm yourself." Before long we'd settled in the break and beverage room. Sister Mary joined us. Nice, hot tea was poured. They were both elderly, gentle, and astute. Short gray hair, pullover sweaters, and pants. "There's a lovely way of folding together the old, old beliefs with the Christianity," Sister Phil continued. "The Celts were tremendously aware of the natural world around them, assigning gods and goddesses to all things. Even the whole country is named after an ancient goddess—Eire."

"Brigid was a woman of the earth, the land," Sister Mary added. "A woman of peace, of hospitality, the woman always reaching out to help the poor. A leader. A healer. These are the qualities we seek to keep alive through teaching about her," she explained.

"Her door was always open," Sister Phil said.

The saint has hundreds of legends attached to her. Like: Everything she cast her eyes upon increased in abundance. For instance, even though she'd given all the butter to the poor, when the master came to claim his, the bucket was overflowing. She turned water into ale (many times). Brigid gave her father's jeweled sword to the beggar man, infuriating her father but inspiring his superiors. And on and on. What the sisters mean by keeping the spirit of St. Brigid alive is this: They hold conferences on peace and on women's rights in developing countries. They offer retreats and hospitality. They organize writing and poetry workshops. The late, great Irish poet John O'Donohue was their friend. He called the Brigidines the Sisters of Light.

Today the retreat center was very quiet. "We are quite exhausted," said Sister Mary. "We just finished a successful three-day conference on human trafficking."

"That's a big topic," I said. They both nodded as if it's just all in a day's work.

The sisters also do something I find amazing: They tend St. Brigid's perpetual flame. In 1993, the Brigidines held an international peace conference. One activity was to take up the flame again, after the hiatus of several hundred years. They lit a torch in the town square, in front of the conference attendees and town officials, and dedicated themselves to keeping it burning. Today that spot next to the tourist office in the town square is marked with a twelve-foot electrically lighted sculpture. I wanted to see the real flame. Would it be in a brass urn, as you sometimes see? Or a gas-fed fire pit? Sister Mary smiled and motioned me to follow her toward the airy meditation room.

"Sister, what is the significance of the flame today?"

"Bringing the light of Jesus," she said. "It's a fragile light and needs to be guarded." In the center of the meditation room, in the middle of the hardwood floor, was a tall votive candle, lit. So simple! It could be on my front hall table. "You see, it's very fragile," Sister Mary repeated. "But not hard to take care of. It lasts about a week, and we relight the new one from the old one." Twenty-seven years seems like a long time to keep your eye on something. "We hope to do it forever," Sister Mary said, and she invited me to sit in one of the chairs that circle the room and spend a bit of time meditating. I sat quietly, the moment seeming cosmic, eternal, deeply privileged, and...*thin.*

When I was finished meditating, I thanked both of them for the tea and the lovely time. Now, sparkling patches of blue shone from between lofty clouds. My coat had dried—had it dried on a sunbeam? That's where St. Brigid once hung her cloak. I headed on foot back into town. Lines from a poem by Elizabeth Barrett Browning fit as I stared at the shining, open fields, the stone ruins of the Black Abbey, and the berry-covered hedges:

> Earth's crammed with heaven,
> And every common bush afire with God;
> But only he who sees, takes off his shoes
> The rest sit round it and pluck blackberries.

I felt like my shoes had floated off a while ago, even as I tromped through the mud. Before I knew it, I was back with Bill at our little place, strategically located next door to the pub. And…the lights never went out in our lodgings.

St. Brigid's Blessing

May Brigid bless the house wherein you dwell
Bless every fireside every wall and door
Bless every heart that beats beneath its roof
Bless every hand that toils to bring it joy
Bless every foot that walks its portals through
May Brigid bless the house that shelters you.

Denice
and Her Grandfather's Third or Fourth Cousin, St. Brother André

One evening, back in 2010, Denice and Guy came over for dinner. Childhood friends of Bill's, they'd moved to LA and found a house two blocks from ours. We became easy couple-friends. On this particular evening, Denice had news to share. She and I poured some wine and settled in the kitchen while the fellows went into the den. Dinner would be out in forty minutes.

"I talked to my mom today. It turns out we're related to a guy who's going to be a saint!" she exclaimed.

"What?"

"Blessed Brother André. My—I think I have this straight—grandfather's third cousin."

My eyes widened. "You have a relative who's going to be canonized? That's amazing!" As if trying to decide whether to go into the whole story, Denice wagged her head a bit and said, "I can't believe it either. Brother André Bessette. My mother's maiden name is Bessette. He died in 1937. Mom never met him, though, because she was just a little girl in Denver. He was in Montreal."

"Denice, how can anyone have a saint as a family member?! That's crazy. When is the canonization?"

"October 10th."

"Let's go! Let's go to Rome. Come on! What an experience!"

Her eyes lit up, but she shook her head no. "I just

can't. I have so much to do," she said slowly.

I simmered down. Truly, Denice did have much to do. I don't know anyone like her. She has a calling to help others. If she isn't busy being of use, she becomes unhappy. So you'll find her at the pool, giving aqua classes to pregnant women. You'll find her visiting an elderly man who has no family—not just now and then but every day, making him brownies to keep his spirits up. In his extreme old age, he'd say, "I love you, Denice." She'd just smile and pat him on the cheek. You'll find her as a St. Vincent de Paul volunteer, following up with a homeless man she's worried about, hunting for him in supermarket parking lots, asking him what he needs. Denice has this capacity to connect. I knew she wouldn't leave all of this for an extravagant trip.

"Okay, okay," I said. "But tell me about him, for heaven's sake. A saint!"

She smiled and relaxed, knowing I wasn't going to pressure her to do something crazy like dash off to Rome. "Well, what my mom said is that he was born in a small town outside Montreal in 1845. He wanted to be a priest, but he was rejected because he wasn't in good health, didn't have very much education, had trouble reading, and most jobs were just too difficult for him. But he was extremely prayerful and very kind. It was his mother who taught him to pray, especially to St. Joseph, who he developed a special devotion for.

"A priest by the name of Father André Provençal took him under his wing and at some point recommended him to the Brothers of the Holy Cross, who ran a men's college, Mount Royal at Notre Dame in

Montreal. In the letter of recommendation to the brothers, Father Provençal said, 'I am sending you a saint.' So, the Brothers of the Holy Cross accepted him and gave him the job of gatekeeper and doorman for the college and the rectory. That's really about all he could do. He greeted everybody. He was supposed to be so warm and loving. He remembered everyone he met. His other job, besides doorman, was listening to the concerns of the sick. He prayed all the time for them."

She paused. We sipped our wine and settled deeper into the easy chairs in the corner of my kitchen. "Pretty soon, more and more people started coming to him for his prayers and his help. Miracles began happening!"

"Really? How come I've never heard of him before?"

"Me either, and I'm related! Healings began. His notoriety spread. I don't know how miracle health cures happen, but they did. There's, like, tons of books written about him. Then, in his dreams, God began telling him to build a church on that spot on Mount Royal. Build a church in honor of St. Joseph."

It took his superiors a long time before they heard Brother André's message to build a church, but at last the church was built. More and more people came each day to have him pray over them. By the early 1900s, it was up into the hundreds per day. When the city of Montreal built a tram to the college, Brother André was given an office at the tram stop. Turns out, the trams were full of people coming up to see him, not to go on into the college.

Denice threw up her hands. "I don't know how this happens, but apparently there are thousands of cures because of him. He never said he did any of them, just that St. Joseph interceded for them. In fact, he never claimed any abilities at all! And here's another amazing thing: When he died, in the middle of winter in 1937, more than a million people showed up to pay respects!"

"I love it, Denice! One million people!"

And now, with my trip earlier this year to Canada, I had the chance to show up for Brother André. To visit what is now the Oratory of St. Joseph, one of Montreal's main tourist and religious sites. I saw the smaller chapel Brother André built, which sits below the magnificent complex that dominates the whole top of Mount Royal today. I saw all the crutches people left after receiving a cure, as God worked through Brother André. From the high terraces of the Oratory, you can see way across the St. Lawrence River—that vista, forever and ever, the premier view of all Montreal.

The Oratory is a maze of chapels and grottoes, a museum with dioramas, and meditation rooms with soft lighting and music. In one of the chapels, you can pray before Brother André's heart. These all surround the main worship space, which is glorious and huge. The afternoon we visited, it was packed with people.

"So I think the main thing about Brother André," Denice concluded when we talked, "is that he was humble. People didn't think he could do much, almost like he was a special-needs person, but really, God used him to do great things."

"That's so wonderful, Denice," I said. "From now on, I get to say I know someone related to a saint." She nodded proudly. We stood up, called Bill and Guy in from the football game, and got dinner out of the oven.

Nine

They Called Me— Lucky

St. Josephine Bakhita
circa 1869–1947
Sudan and Venice

I first learned of this saint when her picture appeared on the cover of a magazine: an African woman dressed in what seemed like rags, with a black-ribboned bonnet, wearing a large medallion. I love that amazing people not from European culture are finally making their way to heights of broader recognition and being made saints. In the photo, St. Josephine Bakhita shows concern. Her large hands rest over her heart. It's impossible to tell what era the picture is from, or that what she was wearing was actually a black and brown sister's habit of the Canossians, an order of nuns known for teaching and missionary work.

She was around nine when Arab slave traders kidnapped her. She cried and wailed so loudly as she was carried away that they derisively told her to shut up and in jest called her Lucky. *Your new name is Lucky—Bakhita, in Arabic*, they told her. The year was 1878. That was it for the little girl from the Darfur village, who just the day before had been playing with her friends in the fields. From there, she would be marched southeast for more than 300 miles and sold two more times before ending up in the slave market of El-Obeid in central Sudan. She'd be forced to convert from her tribal animism to Islam and over twelve years be sold three more times, then given away.

And so Bakhita's life begins at the bottom of the bottom. She couldn't remember her real name but did know she'd come from a loving family, and oh, how her mother had wept when her older sister had been kidnapped the year before. This much, and the fertile look of the land in the southern Sudan, was all she could recall when her autobiography was being written in 1910. She dictated it to a fellow sister at the request of her superiors. It was called *Tale of Wonder*.

In learning about the wonder workers we call saints, I never fail to be awed by their stories. Inspired by their triumph amid wickedness.

Bakhita's first owner was a rich Arab leader. "His house was full of slaves in the flower of their youth. I was given to his daughters. They liked me," she said. But one day she did something wrong and the son beat her almost to death. "I was sent away from that house." Next? Sold to a Turkish general. Bakhita was in full service to his wife and mother. "For three years I was beaten daily, all the while mopping their brows, perfuming them and then laundry— kitchen—fields." One day, the infraction was being present when the master was arguing with his wife. "To take it out on somebody, he ordered me to the courtyard where two of his soldiers flogged me." This left a lifelong giant scar on her leg.

What was a Turkish general doing in the Sudan anyway? Nutshell: In 1518, the Turks conquered Nubia, the northern part of the country. In 1821, the Turco-Egyptian army conquered southern Sudan and founded the city of Khartoum. This created tension with the Islamists. Then Egypt in 1875 gave up its share of the Suez Canal to Britain—more tensions—and Britain banned the slave trade and increased taxes. Even more tensions. Finally, the Islamists declared war, laying siege to Khartoum and controlling it for several decades. Of course, there's more, but that's plenty for now.

The cruel wife of the Turkish general had Bakhita tattooed in a pattern of scars, a miserable custom to identify a slave's owner. She was to bear 114 scar tattoos on her body and arms and legs forever, but the wife did spare her face, as Bakhita was thought to be very beautiful. Possibly the most heartbreaking torture was that the Turkish general did not like Bakhita's breasts, and so on several occasions he squeezed and twisted them to the point of her fainting. He successfully eliminated all fullness. "Now, I am like a table," Bakhita would say late in her life as she was dying, for she never revealed this episode to anyone, out of shame. It only became publicly known during the investigations for her canonization. Bakhita was ever grateful that her virginity was not also robbed of her. It made me feel sick to learn all this. How come some people get born into such terrible circumstances, and so many others, like, say, me or you, come from circumstances of love?

The Turkish general had to flee Kordofan, the city they all lived in, because of rebel invasions. He quickly sold off many slaves but, Bakhita said, "I was among the ten he kept. We mounted camels and fled to Khar-toum. There he said he had slaves to sell." Khartoum at that time was the center of the rubber trade for the world, and Italians had much business there. The Ital-ian consul, Callisto Legnani, came forward. He looked Bakhita over head to toe, and then, she said to her biographer:

> *He asked me to bring him a coffee. He bought me the next day. For two years, I was very happy in their peaceful household. My job was housework. I did not get beaten or scold-ed. The consul was called back to Italy on business. I knew nothing of Italy, but I knew I had to go with him. I knew I had to follow my master to this strange land. Because he liked me so much I dared to ask him to take me. He explained how expensive and long the trip would be. I insisted so much he finally con-sented—and we left. The consul, his business partner Agustino Michieli, a black boy, and me. We traveled by camel, arriving in Sua-kin. We rested a month. We heard the city of Khartoum had fallen to rebels, and all slaves carried off, everything devastated. What if*

*that had been me? We traveled by ship over
the Red Sea, and other seas, and we landed
in Genoa.*

The wife of Mr. Michieli, the consul's friend, met
them at the dock. Turina Michieli looked at Bakhita
and asked her husband why *he* hadn't thought to bring
her a black girl from Africa. "To please his friend, Callisto Legnani gave me to his friend's wife." And just like
that, Bakhita was off with her new owners to a home
near Venice. "I never saw the consul again. Now I was
the nanny to their new baby girl."

After a little while, the Michielis decided to return
to Africa, as they'd bought a large hotel on the newly
opened Suez Canal. Bakhita went with them. It was
thought that she would run the coffee bar of the hotel. After nine months of arranging the hotel's opening,
Mrs. Michieli, their little girl, Mimmina, and Bakhita
returned to Italy to sell all their property and pack up
the furniture. The property was slow to sell, so Turina left Bakhita and little Mimmina temporarily in the
care of the Canossian Sisters in Venice and went to
rejoin her husband in Africa.

Bakhita was only twenty-one when she arrived in
Venice, the miraculous floating city of water and stone.
She was put under the care of the sisters, whose convent was in the shadow of Venice's iconic basilica Santa Maria della Salute (St. Mary of Good Health). Since
the sixteenth century, it has housed the most important icon in the city: a beautiful black Madonna known
as the Madonna of Good Health. For almost 400 years,
Venetians have never failed to celebrate this dark and

gentle image on November 21, with daylong festivities.

Here Bakhita learned of Christianity for the first time. It was a revolution for her to learn that no matter who you are, you are loved by God. The sisters taught her with patience that she was worthy. They taught her with respect and kindness. Well, when Turina Michieli returned a year later to fetch Bakhita and little Mimmina and take them back to the hotel on the Suez Canal, Bakhita would not go. She prayed desperately for the strength to fight for her happiness. She knew it would be "her ruin" to leave the convent. The sisters rallied around Bakhita. Mrs. Michieli was outraged and heartbroken, for they had had genuine affection for each other—but she was mostly outraged and called her well-connected friends and her brother-in-law, a military general. The nuns called on His Eminence the patriarch Domenico Agostini, who turned to the king's attorney general in the matter.

Mrs. Michieli's brother-in-law, the military general, called on the king's attorney general, and for three days a battle royale ensued around the convent of the Canossians. Well, the Italian court ruled that because the British had forced Sudan to outlaw slavery before Bakhita's birth, and because Italy didn't recognize slavery, Bakhita was, in fact, quite free. Weeping with rage and sorrow, Lady Turina left. The emotional toll on Bakhita left her weeping and near collapse as well. But—brighter days ahead!

Venice in February is full of fog and quiet, but confetti sprinkles the stone walkways all over town. It's Carnevale, so the quietness is obliterated when parties and public theatrics pop up. It's neat to know that the entire idea of Carnevale, or Mardi Gras, originated here in the Middle Ages and has since spread to cities everywhere, but Venice is the granddaddy. And despite the rampant exuberance of masks and costumes, drinking and dancing, the fog and the quiet win in the end.

Having exciting friends who pull you along into a larger, freer life is a blessing. Tom and Matt said they were going to Venice, and Bill and I joined them for a few days. I peeled off to do my own thing when I wanted. One morning, I caught a *traghetto* across the Grand Canal, which is like a non-fancy gondola that runs people back and forth across the city's main "street." I wanted to find the convent Bakhita lived in. I had a little Google map printed out that I tried to follow. It took me here, then there, down walkways so narrow my fingertips could touch the buildings on both sides. One walkway opened onto a wider area, and quite by surprise, there it was, a mustard-colored, tile-roofed building, just as it's always been. Nowadays, it's a student dorm. I heard a great quote about Venice: *Being lost is the only place worth visiting in this city.* So don't ask me the names of any of the streets I'd just stumbled along, because I couldn't possibly know. The attached church, with its locked glass front doors, offered me a view of the font where Bakhita was baptized. It's just an average baptismal font, but I loved seeing it. A month after the big fight for her freedom, she was baptized right here and received communion from no less than Archbishop Giuseppe Sarto, the Cardinal Patriarch of Venice, who would later become Pope Pius X. Venice's nobility attended as well, for Bakhita had become a *causa celebre*.

From there I strolled across a tiny footbridge to the wide steps of Santa Maria della Salute. I, like millions of people for centuries before me and as Bakhita had done, kneeled and prayed before the Madonna of Good Health. Bless my life. Bless my dear daughters and my dear husband (who was off shopping for a custom-made shirt). Bless the boys my girls love. And Good St. Jane. Bless my brothers and sisters, those alive and those dead: *Jimmy, Sally, Jeff, Dan, me, Kevin, John, Beth, Michael, Mark*. Bless all of their children, and all of their friends and their friends' children. In fact, bless everybody I know, and then, please, everybody I don't know, especially those born into terrible circumstances. Please don't forget anyone.

These days, when I enter a holy place, what happens is I give a soft "Ohh..." It's like ditching a wet raincoat at the door and coming into a warm room (even though it might actually be freezing), coming into a place of goodness and safety. Funny to think how churches are on so many street corners yet are so often ignored by the harried people passing by. Would society be a little softer and more functional if more people, regardless of their beliefs, availed themselves of these quiet, sacred spaces?

Bakhita's spiritual depths opened. She decided to stay with the Canossian sisters and knew quickly this was to be her new life. The sisters were impressed by her; she was cheerful, she had a big, warm smile, she was funny, she was deeply prayerful. She was so completely open to being of help to all around her that some thought this was because her life as a slave had allowed for nothing but serving others. But her genuine attitude of pleasure in being helpful went beyond that. We all know the difference between being greeted grumpily or with geniality in a restaurant, between working with someone who wants to do a good job as opposed to someone who doesn't care. The way we do something counts.

Bakhita had to endure the open curiosity of all who encountered her. In 1890s Italy, most people had never seen a black person, except in postcards, advertising, or colonial propaganda. She drew a crowd whenever she went out. Little children wanted to lick her hand to see if she was real or chocolate. Adults were a little afraid to shake her hand. She withstood this patiently and even wisecracked about it—like the time when a woman wanted to know why the front of her hand was so black but the palm so white. She said, "Because I live here now!" But eventually she asked her fellow sisters if she could live somewhere where she'd be less in the public eye.

Well, the next day, I set off for the Venice train station to see where that was. My destination was Schio, the small city at the foot of the Dolomites where Bakhita would spend the rest of her life. Schio (*SKI-o*) is calm and wide open, surrounded by fields and foothills. Five years ago, I'd had a meltdown in the Venice train station. Today it was so different! Delightful young people in red smocks were everywhere to help people buy tickets and understand the timetables. It felt like the whole Italian rail system had been sent to charm school. Their attitude of helpfulness was like being given a personal gift by a...well, a *rail system*.

In no time, I was on a quiet, new train headed east into the Veneto—grapes, ruins, and history, right there running past the window. I loved seeing the ancient country villas, all collapsed in on themselves, roof tiles held in place by trees growing up through the centers. In February, the color palette is cool gray and brown. I settled into my seat with a quick prayer of gratitude.

Bakhita's church, convent, and shrine turned out to be a fifteen-minute walk from the Schio train station. Blanca, a young barista at the *caffè* across from the train station, drew me a map on a piece of receipt paper for how to walk there: Go up, pass the Benetton store, turn right at the tree with the bench around it. Pretty soon, through the narrow streets, I would arrive.

It's thrilling to see something you know only from photographs. There it was: the church built to one-third of the proportions of the Pantheon in Rome, with the banner of St. Josephine Bakhita hanging on the front. But the gates were locked. No! Had I misread the website? As I stood there, repeatedly pushing the intercom button on the gate, as if doing it over and over would make it work when it clearly said *Closed*— even in English—a woman hurried by. Brisk and professional, she quickly understood and gestured to me to follow. We went around the block to the back, to the entrance of a busy elementary school, and then I was standing in the reception office. Wizened and arthritic, Sister Reinella looked me over and buzzed for someone who spoke English. Soon Sister Laura, also elderly, and toting a giant bag of rolls from the bakery next door, arrived. The baker gives the sisters all the extra bread. Sister Laura insisted that I put some in my backpack. Okay, in they went, on top of my scarf and iPad. When she heard I'd come all the way from California to learn more about Bakhita, she got a set of keys, even though I was not in her plan. She took me by the arm. "We go together," she said.

She unlocked the church. The two of us stepped into the vast, empty space. "Oh..." I exhaled. There, Bakhita lay in a glass case under the altar. "Not really her body," Sister Laura said in accented English. "And the head and hands are plaster. Her bones, we washed and put in silk bags, in a box, under the habit." We both knelt down. Bakhita's head and hands look really real, but there was a subtle little ridge under her habit that did look like (since I knew) the edge of a box. "She wasn't as tall as she looks here," Sister Laura continued. We looked at her in more of a medical-exam kind of way. "Her arthritis made her much smaller by the end." I nodded, knowing how that can happen.

"But Sister," I asked, "didn't John Paul II take her body back to Sudan, when she was beatified?"

"No, no. She is here. Yes, her arm. He took her arm." And I nodded at that, too, knowing how that can be.

Sister Laura, impossible to tell if she was sixty-five

or eighty-five in her gray Canossian habit, with her clear, brown eyes, was very dear and very all-business. Was she the convent's superior? I followed her out of the church. She took me by the arm, up a flight of terrazzo steps and down a hallway. "We'll go to her bedroom now. But there is the kitchen." She pointed out the window to some windows on the ground floor.

When Bakhita came to the quiet town of Schio in the late 1890s, she was assigned to the kitchen, for she was uneducated and spoke Italian poorly. For two years she looked and learned—and then took over. Just like today, the convent was attached to a school. Amazingly, for the next two years, Bakhita ran a kitchen that turned out three meals a day for one hundred orphan students, plus the paying students, plus the forty nuns. It was said that her food was delicious. It was said that her qualities as a person were radiant in the kitchen—so patient, so willing to do the chores, so joyful, so willing to offer others care and attentiveness.

Bakhita made sure the food not only tasted good but looked beautiful. She decorated the plates with flowers when possible. The fruits were always cut nicely. Bakhita always made sure bowls of soup were kept warm for the sisters who worked late. She had a staff of two other sisters and two girls from the village. The little children just loved her; they followed her, begging for a story, and Bakhita always had time to sit and tell them a tale of her life. She wouldn't go into bad things but told them about the desert, the camels, the Red Sea...well, who doesn't love a good story?

As the years passed and kitchen work became too

much for her, Bakhita was assigned to be the porteress, answering the door to the convent and the school. A doorkeeper, like St. Brother André. Until then, she had largely lived within the confines of the convent, except for a three-year period when she traveled about Italy, escorted by other sisters and urged to speak on behalf of missions in Africa. Now, as porteress, she was in constant contact with people again. Her popularity grew rapidly. Everyone remembered her throaty voice, her jovial laugh, how she greeted all the mothers with babies, the workers, those simply asking for directions. She'd gently chide young women about their makeup or what they wore. She spoke to everyone easily and comfortably, as friends do. Those who spoke with her went away happier, somehow aware that they'd been in the presence of someone great. She offered counsel in bad times and gave small gifts of encouragement, her deep pockets filled with sweets for children. She would say, "My mission here on earth is to help others by praying for them," and even on her deathbed, like St. Kateri, she said, "I am with you always and will pray for you in heaven. I will not leave you."

During World War II, the town of Schio was threatened by Allied bombings, and the citizens prayed fervently to be spared. They wanted to pray with Bakhita because they felt protected just knowing she was with them. God was in charge of the bombers, she said, and "we are mistaken if we tremble." And, in fact, while Schio was bombed, there were no casualties there.

We arrived at Bakhita's bedroom. A narrow, hard bed with a blue-striped cover. A wheelchair fashioned from a regular chair that the gardener had put wheels and a footrest on, reminding me of St. Katharine Drexel. Bakhita's rigged-up chair is in a plexiglass box, because people started picking the straw rush off the seat and taking it. The room is so simple but also so nice— two soft pillows for her head, not a block of wood as St. Teresa of Avila had.

Bakhita prayed without ceasing, especially the rosary, and Eucharistic adoration, and the stations of the cross—continually turning to God as her rescuer and savior. Her devotions were so deep and constant that the other sisters were left with curiosity and admiration. One sister observed that Bakhita was so poor in spirit—which here, I think, means lacking in ego— that she could overlook any insult and the tiny slights that engender resentment in most of us. We've all had experience with getting bothered or swamped in insecurity over a slight or a bit of rudeness. Not to mention getting trapped in looping thoughts: "Why'd she say *that*? How come he did *that*? Why wasn't *I* invited?" It diminishes our ability to bring the love we could.

The sisters who cared for Bakhita during her final illness were horrified when they saw the 114 scar tattoos and the deformed part of her leg. They cried out at how malicious the people were who'd done this to her. Bakhita replied, "Those poor souls were not bad; they did not know the Lord and did not know how much harm they were doing to me. They were masters, and I was their slave. Just as we are in the habit of doing good, the slave traders and owners did that out of habit, not out of wickedness."

This is a lot to accept. But remember when John Paul II almost died of an assassin's bullets? Back in 1981, while he was greeting crowds in St. Peter's Square? The would-be murderer was Mehmet Agca. Despite his blood loss, John Paul II asked Catholics around the world to pray for Agca. In 1983, the pope visited him in jail. They had a private conversation, and it was reported that they emerged as friends! John Paul II even asked for Agca's pardon in 2000, which Agca received, but then was deported to Turkey to finish another prison sentence for murder. Well, incredibly, in 2014, when Mehmet Agca was released from Turkish prison, he traveled back to Rome and laid two dozen white roses on the pontiff's tomb. Now that's a healing.

So, what is Bakhita's message to us? According to Father Divo Barsotti, a theologian, she is proof that one's life can be transformed from non-personhood and enslavement into a state of dignity, strength, and emotional and spiritual freedom. Bakhita had the option to be a fragmented personality ruled by despair and resentment, but through faith she found a different way. She actually let go of her personal injuries to rewrite her entire life narrative as being, in fact, deeply lucky and deeply grateful.

Outside her bedroom were display cases, things from her culture when she was a girl: fearsome masks, a hand tool, a ceremonial rattle. Could arriving in Venice in 1890 have been more strange for her? Right next to that display case was another, with a suitcase and umbrella that looked exactly like Mary Poppins's. What extreme culture clash, right? When Bakhita died, people from far and wide came to pay respects to Madre Morretta, the Brown Mother. She lay in an open coffin for two days as people filed past, yet her body remained warm, her lips pink, her arms soft. This amazed and frightened the doctors. She remained just like that until they finally agreed it really was time to close the lid.

Her achievements? She was a cook and a porter-ess in a quiet convent in the Italian countryside. The thousands of children she cooked for remembered her all their lives, and when interviewed in their eight-ies for the canonization process, they remembered detailed conversations and impressions. "I loved how she smelled." "I always wanted to sit next to her." "She would sit down and say, 'Now, children, did I tell you how the stars look in Africa?' " Bakhita was the master of the small act. She did not carry the scars of her past. She purified her memory through forgiveness. Sister Laura said that at her death, the convent received a call requesting that they not throw anything of hers away. No toothbrushes or scissors or underwear even. People knew she was going to be a saint.

Bakhita was beatified in 1992 by Pope John Paul II, the pope who'd helped bring down the Iron Curtain. At her canonization he said of her, "She most perfectly lived the modernness of the Beatitudes." He called the Beatitudes the identity card of Christians.

Wait. The Beatitudes. This sent me to the Bible I had recently bought at a bookstand at the Burbank Airport. For me, the airport was the perfect place to buy myself a Bible. I would have been scared off by a religious bookstore. This one was displayed next to *1,000 Places to Visit Before You Die*. I had never owned a Bible before, and buying it at an airport magazine stand felt like I wasn't taking too big a plunge. Strange, I know, but I was raised on a catechism and, until recently, my interests hadn't leaned toward Bible study.

Of course. The Beatitudes. The list of characteristics Jesus instructed us to aspire to in his Sermon on the Mount. Really, though, they are a little hard to understand. Take "Blessed are the meek, for they shall inherit the earth." *Meek* to me, for today's woman, doesn't seem like a good word. I know it's me and not Jesus, so I started asking around. For a few months, I asked all kinds of people what they thought meek meant. Boy, do we live in a tower of Babel!

My friend Lynn, a lifelong feminist, took me strolling along the bike path of the Hood River, which courses through Portland, where she lives. Old friends, we strolled like philosophers past the pocket parks, the cafés, the kayak clubs. "Lynn, what do you think the word *meek* means?"

"That's the word that keeps women down," she answered.

"But wait, as in 'the meek shall inherit the earth'? "

Lynn paused. Me, too. "I don't know," she continued. "Maybe it used to mean something else, but I definitely don't see it as a positive."

In Minneapolis, Bill and I strolled through his cousin Betsy's tree-shaded neighborhood. I posed it to them both: "What do you guys make of the word *meek*?"

Betsy answered instantly: "Someone who doesn't

speak up."

"But how does that give you the earth?" I wanted to know.

Bill added, "No, *meek* means those who don't have power. Those who are put down or are too weak. Those who don't have a voice."

In Anacortes, my sister Bethie and I walked the marina, looking at all the pleasure boats, looking for hers, which she wanted to show me. A rare blue heron perched on a post followed us with his bead-yellow eyes. "Bethie, is the word *meek* a positive or a negative?"

"Hmm. *Meek*. I think it means introverted. Not bossy. Letting others get their way."

In the end, I think my friend Sherrillee got it pretty right: "Not thinking you are better than others. Leaving room so others can speak."

As we all know, the Sudan has seen so much poverty, war, drought, hunger, and human displacement. As a way to shine light on this, after her beatification, John Paul II personally accompanied the relics of Mother Bakhita, bringing them back to the people of Sudan. In Khartoum, the people's welcome was as effusive as any he ever received. He said it reminded him of his first return to Poland. A crowd of 300,000 lined the roads from the airport to the city. He offered an immense, open-air Mass to honor the official return of Bakhita to her homeland. People flew banners saying, "Pope, give us hope" and "God created all men equal." John Paul II said St. Bakhita had the power to evoke great change in Africa.

Indeed, the spirit of this humble woman is now

spreading around the world. Today more than a hundred youth groups, hospitals, schools, parishes, and medical dispensaries across Africa bear her name, along with at least two religious communities. In Italy, two migrant centers are associated with her. She is present in Brazil, Argentina, Mexico, and Washington, DC.

Sister Laura had been so generous with her time, but now I was checking my watch. I had to catch a three o'clock train back. She read my actions. "Before you go," she said, "maybe you would like this." She reached into a drawer and took out a tiny yellow plastic envelope. I opened it and smiled broadly. Inside was a relic of Bakhita's—a round piece of her clothing, just the size of a bit of confetti. This is a second-class relic, a piece of a saint's clothing.

"Sister Laura, thank you so much. I love it!" I closed my hand around the little envelope. As I took my leave of the elderly sisters at the Canossian convent on Via Fusinato, at the foot of the Dolomites, I felt joyful and grateful. My travels had taken me into the mystery of so many different people's searches for connection and meaning and purpose. We look to God for His guidance, and we find it in our own myriad ways. Me, by hopping a train or a plane and thinking I'm going somewhere far, but really finding I'm just going inward—which is, as it turns out, a pretty big place.

It's where Good St. Jane and Ruthie are—lively as ever. It's where friends jump to mind in an instant. It's where I conjure wonderful plans for some new adventure. It's where the tales from the other decades of my life line the halls and step forward whenever I want, making me laugh out loud. This is a lot to keep busy with, right? But it's peanuts compared with the vast field of God that also stretches within, where clouds are stepping-stones, where my heart feels more like lungs with wings, which can expand and expand and, even then, expand some more.

I walked back to the train station thinking about the desire to be with and of and for God. The paths we travel, lit with a soft or a strong light from the people we travel with, leading us, hopefully, ever closer. Bakhita didn't build hundreds of schools or give vast fortunes away. She just brought joy, comfort, and good food to the people around her, and she shared herself thoroughly with others—something within reach for the yous and mes of the world. Bakhita, with all her humbleness, has shown us how the worst possible life, with God as her lamp, became the best possible life.

Epilogue

If I had had a crystal ball through the carefree travels I enjoyed in the writing of this book, even being in Italy right on the eve of the 2020 coronavirus pandemic, surely my prayers before the tombs of the wonderful people whose lives I've explored would have gone more like, "Protect us from this thief in the night, imbue our doctors and nurses with superhuman energy, give our researchers divine inspiration in their quest for answers. And loss, so much loss and upheaval. Protect us all in the storms of change...." These are the prayers needed as I write this.

The saints were excellent first responders. Many were medics and nurses during the epidemics of their day. They showed themselves to be fearless, stepping into frightful situations, bringing calm where panic prevailed. They knew how to keep their eyes on God, on His kingdom. This is what they instruct us to do.

So, let us pick up the pieces and set our eyes on the horizon of a new day. We have helpers in the somehow saints all around us. And what I really hope, for myself and for you, is that each of us can take a step toward creating more love in our world. I see us laughing, with our sleeves rolled up, creating love, the way one creates art or makes bread or plans a party—making tangible love through our actions. Bringing it. Spreading it around. Just deciding *this situation needs more love*—and shazam! You've made things bloom.

Bringing love has endless interpretations, but it's got a uniform outcome: You are better, and others are better for it. It allows the "big version" of you to emerge. That's all any of us could possibly be, our own big version of our own self. That is what this time requires of us. The saints offer example after example of how to find new depths, greater capacities, stronger energy—even when you think you've got nothing. Even when you believe you are limited by your age. By praying and working with the phrase "Believe more in God's power than in your weakness," I began to be able to lift myself. And are we not taught that God is just waiting to give us our heart's desire? God doesn't say "You are too old to do that" or "You are too young to do that"—to achieve what is there, waiting in your heart. No, He is there hoping you will get around to being all He had planned for you.

And so, another set of travels ends. I look at all the research books piled up under my worktable. How memorable the lives of these saints are! They figured out
how to improve themselves to the point of becoming
great gifts to humanity, people we can look to as we
work on creating the big version of ourselves. They're
my friends and helpers on the real journey I'm on, of
just getting better at living—of being able to, what?
I suppose to fully come to the party of what each day
is, taking everything I can from each sixteen hours of
awake time, shazaming-up fun and satisfaction and
ways to help, somehow, those around me. And the
only way I know to do this is to put all of it into God's
hands. And get busy doing it.

No matter how dark the darkness,
it cannot extinguish the light
from a single flame.

— ST. FRANCIS OF ASSISI

Acknowledgments

First and foremost, I am grateful to you, the reader, for taking precious time to buy, read, and talk about *Saint Everywhere*, the foundation for the book you now hold. Your support was the energy that revved the engine for this effort. I'm grateful for the ridiculous or poignant childhood memories that made their way into these pages. And I'm deeply grateful for the ability to sit down and get to work, taking the ideas in my head and shaping them into chapters.

All of the above depends on the generosity and willingness of a few great people. Colleen Dunn Bates, my publisher, posed the annoying question, "What do you want to write next?" two weeks after *Saint Everywhere* came out. I was still in a state of amazement that it had been published and could only say, "I don't know." But I kind of *did* know. I wanted to keep being able to tell the saints' stories. I loved hearing comments from my readers like, "I've started praying again." Or, "My friend, who is sick, just loved it." I said to Colleen, "What about a sequel?" She gave me a businesswoman's stare and said, "Could you get it ready for Christmas?" I took a breath and answered, "I'll do my best." So a huge thank-you to Colleen as well as to her team: cover designer David Ter-Avanesyan, layout designer Amy Inouye, copy editor Leilah Bernstein, and staff Caitlin Ek, Katelyn Keating, and Julianne Johnson.

And then Janet Nippell swooped in like an angel and said, "I promised to edit anything you write, Mary Lea. I'll go again." As the chapters added up, she put her other work aside and helped me over the rocky terrain of shaping and polishing.

Illustrator Joe Rohde happily came on board again. "This time, let's switch up the style," he said, instantly engaged. He is such a professional that he can work anywhere, be it his office at Disney or the kitchen table or on an airplane headed to Bhutan.

Let me call out to my prayer sisters, my ongoing group of friends. For almost twenty-five years we've met every month, helping one another deepen our spirituality and our appreciation for the journey of life we are embarked upon. Special acknowledgments to Judy McCord, who has facilitated our meetings. She is ten to fifteen years older than most of us, and ten times wiser.

A prayer-filled thank-you to each of the individuals who found themselves in the "little chapters" that cushion the big chapters of the various saints. You are testaments to the fact that we often do not know the impressions we leave on one another.

And last but not least, I want to acknowledge Bill. We've always said that God had a sense of humor when he put us together. Even when I'm standing on a chair, I'm still only as tall as his chin. His outlook on life is all facts 'n' figures, while I'm pretty much *Who cares, let's do it anyway*. And for all these thirty-five years, he has been my companion and my protector. He is the father to the best gifts the universe could give: my children. And, lucky me, he's great with a map.

I added a short phrase to my autograph, which I've used hundreds of times when signing books, and I mean it with all my heart: *Keep bringing love.*

About the Author

MARY LEA CARROLL is a writer and storyteller whose debut book, *Saint Everywhere*, was published in 2019. Before raising children, she worked in travel, in the theater, and in Hollywood. While raising her children, she taught children's creative writing and helped her husband in his motion-picture advertising business. A contributor to the book *Hometown Pasadena* and a graduate of San Francisco State, she is a lifelong resident of Pasadena, California.

About the Illustrator

JOE ROHDE is an executive designer at Walt Disney Imagineering.